XI

MSL
TAXN
TOL

Tolley's Corporation Tax Post-Budget Supplement

D0314866

2 Bunhill Row
London
EC1Y 8HQ

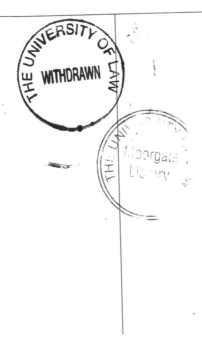

The University of Law

incorporating The College of Law

This book must be returned to the library on or before the last date
stamped below. Failure to do so will result in a fine.

Bloomsbury Library
T: 01483 216387
library-bloomsbury@law.ac.uk

Moorgate Library
T: 01483 216371
library-moorgate@law.ac.uk

Tolley's Corporation Tax 2017 Post-Budget Supplement

by

Lisa-Jane Harper BSc MA ATT CTA ADIT

Kevin Walton MA

Members of the LexisNexis Group worldwide

United Kingdom	RELX (UK) Limited trading as LexisNexis, 1–3 Strand, London WC2N 5JR
Australia	Reed International Books Australia Pty Ltd trading as LexisNexis, Chatswood, New South Wales
Austria	LexisNexis Verlag ARD Orac GmbH & Co KG, Vienna
Benelux	LexisNexis Benelux, Amsterdam
Canada	LexisNexis Canada, Markham, Ontario
China	LexisNexis China, Beijing and Shanghai
France	LexisNexis SA, Paris
Germany	LexisNexis Deutschland GmbH, Munster
Hong Kong	LexisNexis Hong Kong, Hong Kong
India	LexisNexis India, New Delhi
Italy	Giuffrè Editore, Milan
Japan	LexisNexis Japan, Tokyo
Malaysia	Malayan Law Journal Sdn Bhd, Kuala Lumpur
Mexico	LexisNexis Mexico, Mexico
New Zealand	LexisNexis NZ Ltd, Wellington
Singapore	LexisNexis Singapore, Singapore
South Africa	LexisNexis, Durban
USA	LexisNexis, Dayton, Ohio

© 2017 RELX (UK) Ltd

Published by LexisNexis
This is a Tolley title

ISBN for this volume: 9780754553700

Printed and bound in Great Britain by Hobbs the Printers Ltd, Totton, Hampshire

Visit LexisNexis at www.lexisnexis.co.uk.

About This Supplement

This Supplement to Tolley's Corporation Tax 2016/17 gives details of changes in the law and practice of capital gains tax and corporation tax on chargeable gains from 2 September 2016 to 7 March 2017. It lists the changes in the same order and under the same paragraph headings as the annual publication. Also included is a summary of the Chancellor's Budget proposals made on 8 March 2017.

Each time Tolley's Corporation Tax 2016/17 is used, reference should be made to the material contained in this Supplement. The Contents give a list of all the chapters and paragraphs which have been updated.

Contents

Contents

Contents

Spring Budget 2017

1

Introduction: Charge to Tax, Rates and Profit Computations

Tax powers in Northern Ireland

[1.3] The following text is added at the end.

'Draft legislation was published in December 2016 which will give all small and medium-sized enterprises trading in Northern Ireland the potential to benefit from the Northern Ireland rate of corporation tax. This will permit all SMEs which do not meet the Northern Ireland employment test, but do have a trading presence there, to access the rate on the same terms as large companies. The changes will come into force on Royal Assent to Finance Bill 2017 and have effect when the rate comes into force.

See www.gov.uk/government/publications/finance-bill-2017-draft- legislation-overvi ew-documents/overview-of-legislation-in-draft and www.gov.uk/govern ment/public ations/northern-ireland-rate-of-corporation-tax-changes-to-small -and-medium-size d-enterprise-regime/northern-ireland-rate-of-corporation-tax-changes-to-small-and -med ium-sized-enterprise-regime.'

5

Anti-Avoidance

Introduction to anti-avoidance

[5.1] The paragraph immediately before the heading 'Repayment claims in avoidance cases' is deleted.

Anti-avoidance case law

[5.2] The last paragraph on page 49 and the first two paragraphs on page 50 are amended to read as follows.

'Two recent cases highlight the application of purposive construction by the courts, and its limitations. In *Hancock and Hancock v HMRC* FTT, [2014] UKFTT 695 (TC) the taxpayers sold shares for loan notes. The notes were not QCBs (for CGT purposes) as they were redeemable in a foreign currency. A smaller tranche of loan notes were issued as deferred consideration, which were later amended to remove the foreign currency redemption clause (so as to become QCBs). All the loan notes were then converted into new loan notes, which were QCBs, which were then redeemed. As QCBs are exempt there are provisions at *TCGA 1992, s 116* to cover scenarios when a non-QCB is converted into a QCB, so as to hold over the gain on the non-QCB at the date of conversion. The taxpayers argued this only applied where the assets being converted are exclusively non-QCBs, in this instance the loan notes were a mix of QCBs and non-QCBs. The First-tier Tribunal found for the taxpayers. By removing the foreign currency clause to mix up QCBs and non-QCBs a reduced CGT charge resulted on the share sale. HMRC argued there were two distinct conversions, or by applying the *Ramsay* doctrine only the original loan notes were redeemed. However, whilst the tribunal acknowledged the intention to exploit a loophole to avoid CGT, it noted that no purposive construction could fill this gap, and that *Ramsay* could not cure the defect by disregarding the reality of the conversion.

This can be contrasted with *Chappell v HMRC* CA, [2016] STC 1980. The taxpayer had entered into a marketed scheme under which manufactured payments were made under a loan of securities. The CA found there was no commercial or other purpose to the arrangements except avoiding tax through a deduction for the manufactured payments. The loan notes, interest paid and manufactured payments were all created for the purposes of the scheme and were self-cancelling with no practical significance. This was held to be sufficient to deprive them of their essential characteristics for the purposes of the legislation and so this resulted in no deduction for the taxpayer. This contrasts with the *Hancock* case, where there was some commercial content and reason for the transaction. In *Chappell* the taxpayer started with nothing and ended with nothing.

In *Steven Price v HMRC* [2015] UKUT 164 (TCC) the Upper Tribunal found that a capital loss scheme failed under the *Ramsay* principle. The success of the scheme relied on the participants having spent large sums on acquiring assets and then realising very small amounts on their disposal. In its judgment the Upper Tribunal referred to *Collector of Stamp Revenue v Arrowtown Assets Ltd* [2003] HKCFA 46 and stressed the requirements to 'construe statutory provisions purposively' and to 'view transactions realistically'. The Upper Tribunal approved of the lower tribunal's approach when asking the question: what did the taxpayer pay for? He had not outlaid £6 million for some 'worthless shares'. The Upper Tribunal also agreed with the lower tribunal's conclusion that the subscription for shares in this case had not been an isolated transaction, but had formed part of a composite and pre-planned series of steps.'

General anti-abuse rule

[5.3] A new paragraph is added immediately before the heading 'Definitions' to read as follows.

'HMRC do not give formal or informal clearances that the GAAR does not apply. As part of its engagement with large businesses and wealthy individuals, however, HMRC does discuss commercial arrangements and confirms where appropriate that it doesn't regard particular arrangements as tax avoidance. See www.gov.uk/govern ment/collections/seeking-clearance-or-approval-for-a-transacti on.'

Land sold and leased back — payments connected with transferred land

[5.7] The fourth paragraph is amended to read as follows.

'Specifically, where land (or any interest or estate in land) is transferred (by sale, lease, surrender or forfeiture of lease etc.) and, as a result of:

- a lease of the land, or any part of it, granted at the time of transfer or subsequently by the transferee to the transferor; or

- another transaction or transactions affecting the land or interest or estate,

the transferor, or a company associated (see below) with the transferor, becomes liable to make a payment of rent under a lease of the land or part of it (including any premium treated as rent — see 60.10 PROPERTY INCOME), or any other payment connected with the land or part of it (whether it is a payment of rentcharge or other payment under some other transaction), which would be allowable as a deduction:

- in computing trading profits;
- in computing the profits of a UK property business;
- in computing profits or income under any of the provisions listed at *CTA 2010, s 1173* (miscellaneous income) or in computing losses for which relief is available under *CTA 2010, s 91* (see 51.9 LOSSES);
- under *CTA 2009, s 1219* (management expenses of a company's investment business — see 45.3 INVESTMENT COMPANIES AND INVESTMENT BUSINESS); or
- under *FA 2012, s 76* for accounting periods beginning on or after 1 January 2013, previously *ICTA 1988, s 76* (expenses of insurance companies); then

the deduction for tax purposes in respect of the rent or other payment is limited to the 'commercial rent' of the land to which it relates for the period for which the payment is made. In fact, the position is judged on a cumulative basis.'

The statutory reference at the end is amended to read as follows.

'[*CTA 2010, ss 834–848*].'

Hybrid and other mismatches

[5.14] The following text is added at the end.

'Future developments

Small amendments will be made to the hybrid mismatch rules in the Finance Bill 2017 in order to make sure they operate as intended. In particular, the requirement to make a claim for an accounting period to be permitted is to be removed. This is in order to reduce the compliance burden as this requirement could otherwise lead to a very high number of individual claims, due to the large volume of financial instruments that are likely to fall within the scope of the hybrid mismatch rules. In addition, amortisation is no longer to be treated as a relevant deduction for certain of the deduction/non-inclusion cases. These changes will apply from 1 January 2017, from the commencement of the regime.

See www.gov.uk/government/publications/corporation-tax-changes-to-the-hy brid-a nd-other-mismatches-regime-technical-note/corporation-tax-minor-changes-to-the-hy brid-and-other-mismatches-regime-technical-note.'

6

Appeals

Failure to comply with rules

[6.17] The following paragraph is added before the statutory reference at the end.

'An attempt to have HMRC barred from taking any part in a case was unsuccessful in *Foulser v HMRC* FTT 2011, [2012] SFTD 94. On appeal to the Upper Tribunal, however, the case was remitted for rehearing by the FTT ([2013] STC 917). An attempt to have HMRC barred also failed in *Ritchie v HMRC* [2016] UKFTT 509 (TC), 2016 STI 2753.'

Award of costs

[6.28] The following paragraph is added before the statutory references at the end.

'Partially successful appellants were ordered to pay two-thirds of HMRC's costs in *Bastionspark LLP v HMRC* UT, [2016] STC 2549.'

7

Assessments

Discovery

[7.3] The second and the third paragraph on page 174 are amended to read as follows.

'In *Pattullo v HMRC* UT, [2016] STC 2043 a discovery assessment was issued in respect of tax planning which was the subject of a different case progressing through the courts. The Tribunal held that a discovery could only occur once that similar case's appeal was final, because it was only at that point in time that what had only been a suspicion on the part of the tax officer was converted to the positive view that there was an insufficiency of tax. In *Michael Yin v HMRC* FTT, [2014] UKFTT 865 (TC) the Tribunal held that HMRC were correct to wait until the expiry of the appeal period for the direction notice before issuing the discovery assessments (which was the only way of assessing the taxpayer's income). The amount of under-assessed income was only 'discovered' at that point.

In *Terence Lynch v NCA* FTT, [2014] UKFTT 1088 (TC) the First-tier Tribunal found that the National Crime Agency (NCA) had been entitled to raise discovery assessments. The Tribunal found that the NCA had reasonable grounds to suspect there was a charge to income tax as a result of criminal conduct (under the *Proceeds of Crime Act 2002*); and that the conditions for a discovery assessment under *TMA 1970, s 29* were met: unexplained bank deposits were missing from the tax return, which the tax officer would not have been aware of at the end of the enquiry period, and the 20–year time limit applied (in cases of such deliberate concealment). In *John Martin v HMRC* [2015] UKUT 161 the Upper Tribunal found that the issue of a confiscation order (under the Proceeds of Crime Act 2002) did not preclude HMRC from raising a discovery assessment on the basis of what HMRC believed to have been Mr Martin's profits to build and maintain a house and his lifestyle.'

8

Banks

Bank Levy

[8.11] The table on page 192 is amended to read as follows.

The Bank Levy rates are as follows:

	Short-term chargeable liabilities	Long-term chargeable equity and liabilities
1.1.21 onwards	0.100%	0.050%
1.1.20–31.12.20	0.140%	0.070%
1.1.19–31.12.19	0.150%	0.075%
1.1.18–31.12.18	0.160%	0.080%
1.1.17–31.12.17	**0.170%**	**0.085%**
1.1.16–31.12.16	0.180%	0.090%
1.4.15–31.12.15	0.210%	0.105%
1.1.14–31.3.15	0.156%	0.078%
1.1.13–31.12.13	0.130%	0.065%
1.1.12–31.12.12	0.088%	0.044%
1.4.11–31.12.11	0.075%	0.0375%
1.3.11–31.3.11	0.100%	0.050%
1.1.11–28.2.11	0.050%	0.025%

The list of statutory references at the end is amended to read as follows.

'[FA 2011, s 73, Sch 19; FA 2013, ss 202–205; FA 2014, ss 119, 120, Sch 26; FA 2015, s 76; F(No 2)A 2015, s 20(1)–(8), Sch 2; FA 2016, s 56(10)–(15); SI 2011 No 1785; SI 2016 No 874].'

11

Capital Allowances on Plant and Machinery

First-year allowances

[11.13] The list on page 275 is amended to read as follows.

'(a)   by any person on **'energy-saving plant or machinery'** (see **11.16** below) which is unused and not second-hand, in which case the maximum FYA is **100%**;

(b)   by any person on **'environmentally beneficial plant or machinery'** (see **11.17** below), unused and not second-hand, in which case the maximum FYA is **100%** (but long-life asset expenditure, see **11.32** below, does not qualify);

(c)   **before 1 April 2021** by any person on cars first registered after 16 April 2002 which are either **'electrically-propelled'** or have **'low CO_2 emissions'** (see

11.18 below), and which are unused and not second-hand, in which case the maximum FYA is **100%**;

(d) **before 1 April 2018** by any person on plant or machinery, unused and not second-hand, installed at a **'gas refuelling station'** (see **11.19** below) for use solely for or in connection with refuelling vehicles with natural gas, biogas or hydrogen fuel, in which case the maximum FYA is **100%**;

(e) by a company on plant or machinery for use wholly for the purposes of a 'ring fence trade' within *CTA 2010, s 330(1)* (**petroleum extraction activities**), in which case the maximum FYA is **100%**; (the FYA is withdrawn where the plant etc. is not used in such a trade, or is used for some other purpose, within the five years after the expenditure is incurred — see *CAA 2001, s 45G*);

(f) **after 31 March 2010 and before 1 April 2018** by any person on **'zero-emission goods vehicles'**, unused and not second-hand, in which case the maximum FYA is **100%**; this is subject to exclusions and to a monetary limit on the total FYAs of this type that can be claimed by any person; see **11.20** below. Pursuant to *FA 2014, s 64* the Treasury may by order extend this period of availability;

(g) **after 31 March 2012** by a company on the provision of unused (not second-hand) plant or machinery for use primarily in an area which (at the time the expenditure is incurred) is a 'designated assisted area'. The expenditure must be incurred in the period of eight years beginning with the date on which the area is (or is treated as) designated and there are exclusions and a monetary limit on the total FYAs of this type that can be claimed by any person in respect of any one investment project in any area; see **11.21** below.'

The last two paragraphs are amended to read as follows.

'[*CAA 2001, ss 39, 45A, 45AA, 45B–45D, 45DA, 45DB, 45E–45N, 50, 52, 52A, 268A–268C, Sch 3 paras 14, 48–50; F(No 3)A 2010, Sch 7 paras 2–3, 5, 7; FA 2013, ss 68(1), 69; FA 2014, s 64; SI 2015 No 60; FA 2015, s 45; FA 2016, s 69; SI 2016 No 984*].

Simon's Taxes. See B3.320–326, B3.330.'

The following paragraph is added at the end.

'A 100% first-year capital allowance will be introduced in Finance Bill 2017 for expenditure incurred in the period from 23 November 2016 to 31 March 2019 on new, unused electric charge-point equipment installed solely for the purpose of charging electric vehicles. See www.gov.uk/government/publications/capital-allowances-first-year-allowance-for-electric-charge-points.'

Energy-saving plant or machinery

[11.16] The list of statutory references at the end is amended to read as follows.

'[*CAA 2001, ss 45A, 45AA, 45B, 45C; FA 2012, s 45(2)(3); FA 2013, s 67; SI 2001 No 2541; SI 2009 No 1863; SI 2010 No 2286; SI 2011 No 2221; SI 2012 No 1832; SI 2013 No 1763; SI 2015 No 1508; SI 2016 No 927*].'

Environmentally beneficial plant or machinery

[11.17] The list of statutory references at the end is amended to read as follows.

'[*CAA 2001, s 45H–45J; SI 2003 No 2076; SI 2009 No 1864; SI 2010 No 2483; SI 2011 No 2220; SI 2012 Nos 1838, 2602; SI 2013 No 1762; SI 2015 No 1509; SI 2016 No 952*].'

Energy-efficient cars

[**11.18**] The text is amended to read as follows.

'For the purposes of **11.13**(c) above, a car has 'low CO_2 emissions' if it is first registered on the basis of a qualifying emissions certificate (see *CAA 2001, s 268C*) and has CO_2 emissions (see *CAA 2001, s 268C*) of 75g/km or less (50g/km for expenditure incurred on or after 1 April 2018). Previously, for expenditure incurred before 1 April 2015 the limit was 95g/km or less; for expenditure incurred before 1 April 2013, it was 110g/km or less. A car is '*electrically-propelled*' if it is propelled solely by electrical power derived from an external source or from a storage battery not connected to any source of power when the car is in motion. See also HMRC Capital Allowances Manual CA23153. [*CAA 2001, s 45D; FA 2013, s 68(1)(5); SI 2015 No 60; SI 2016 No 984*].

Simon's Taxes. See **B3.324A**.'

Special rate expenditure

[**11.26**] The final paragraph under the heading 'Cars' is amended to read as follows.

'A car has '*low CO_2 emissions*' if, when first registered, it was registered on the basis of a qualifying emissions certificate (as defined by *CAA 2001, s 268C*) and its CO_2 emissions (see *CAA 2001, s 268C*) do not exceed 130g/km. For expenditure incurred on or after 1 April 2018 the limit will be 110g/km. Previously, for expenditure incurred before 1 April 2013, the limit was160g/km. '*Car*' is as defined by *CAA 2001, s 268A* (see **11.12**(ii) above) and excludes a motor cycle.'

The list of statutory references before the heading 'Long-life asset expenditure — transitional' is amended to read as follows.

'[*CAA 2001, ss 65(1), 104A, 104AA, 104B–104D, 104G; FA 2010, s 28(6)(7)(9)(10); FA 2011, s 10(3)(a)(4)(8)–(13); FA 2012, s 45(4); FA 2013, s 68(3)(6)(8); SI 2016 No 984*].'

Renewals basis

[**11.79**] The second paragraph is amended to read as follows.

'For expenditure incurred before 1 April 2016, replacements and alterations of trade tools (meaning any implement, utensil or article) were allowable deductions notwithstanding the fact that the expenditure would otherwise be capital. [*CTA 2009, s 68; FA 2016, s 72(1)(4)(5)*]. Replacement of parts is allowed under general principles so far as the identity of the plant or machinery is retained.'

13

Capital Gains — Groups

Change of a company's nature

[13.28A] A new section is added as follows.

'If:

(a)   within any period of three years, a company becomes a member of a group of companies and there is (either earlier or later in that period, or at the same time) 'a major change in the nature or conduct of a trade or business' carried on by that company immediately before it became a member of that group, or

(b)   at any time the scale of the activities in a trade or business carried on by a company has become small or negligible, and before any considerable revival of the trade or business, that company becomes a member of a group of companies,

the trade or business carried on before that change, or which has become small or negligible, is disregarded for the purposes of **13.28**(c) above in relation to any time before the company became a member of the group in question.

'*A major change in the conduct of a trade or business*' includes a reference to a major change in services or facilities provided or a major change in customers or, in the case of a company with investment business, a major change in the nature of investments held. Regard will also be had to appropriate changes in other factors such as the location of the company's business premises, the identity of the company's suppliers, management or staff, the company's methods of manufacture, or the company's pricing or purchasing policies to the extent that these factors indicate that a major change has occurred. Efficiency changes and technological advancements would not in themselves indicate that a major change in the nature or conduct of a trade or business has occurred.

HMRC will compare any two points in three years which include the date of change of ownership of the company. This applies even if the change is the result of a gradual process which began outside the period of three years mentioned in (a) above. HMRC take note of both qualitative and quantitative issues as discussed in the cases *Willis v Peeters Picture Frames Ltd* CA (NI) 1982, 56 TC 436 and *Purchase v Tesco Stores Ltd* Ch D 1984, 58 TC 46 respectively (HMRC Statement of Practice 10/91).

Where the operation of the above provisions depends on circumstances or events at a time after the company becomes a member of any group of companies (but not more than three years after), an assessment to give effect to the provisions may be made within six years from that time or the latest such time.

[*TCGA 1992, Sch 7A para 8; FA 2016, s 55*].'

14

Capital Gains — Substantial Shareholdings

Introduction to capital gains — substantial shareholdings

[14.1] The following text is added at the end.

'A number of changes are to be made to the conditions which must be met for the substantial shareholdings exemption to apply, with effect for disposals on or after 1 April 2017. The changes are as follows:

(a)   the condition that the investing company must be a trading company or part of a trading group will be removed;

(b)   the condition that the investment must have been held for at least a continuous period of 12 months in the two years preceding the sale will be extended to a continuous period of 12 months in the six years preceding the sale; and

(c)   the condition that the company whose shares are sold continues to be a qualifying company immediately after the sale will be withdrawn, except where the sale is to a connected party.

The exemption will also apply where the company whose shares are sold is not a trading company if it is owned by qualifying institutional investors (as defined). Full exemption will apply if at least 80% of the ordinary share capital is owned by such investors. Proportionate exemption will apply where between 25% and 80% is owned by such investors.

In addition, where the exemption relating to companies owned by qualifying institutional investors applies, the substantial shareholding condition may be met if the investing company's shareholding is below 10% of the ordinary share capital but cost more than £50 million.

See www.gov.uk/government/publications/reform-of-substantial-shareholding-exemption-for-qualifying-institutional-investors.'

15

Charities

Introduction to charities

[15.1] The following paragraph is added at the end.

'**Contributions to grassroots sports**

From 1 April 2017, companies will be able to claim a corporation tax deduction for contributions made for charitable purposes to grassroots sports. There will be no cap on payments made to recognised sports governing bodies, however payments made directly to grassroots sports institutions will be restricted to a £2,500 annual deduction.

See www.gov.uk/government/publications/corporation-tax-deductions-for-contributions-to-grassroots-sport.'

Restrictions on exemptions

[15.9] The list under the heading 'Non-charitable expenditure' on page 468 is amended to read as follows.

'(a) any trading loss other than in charitable trade or it qualifies under the small trade, fund raising or lotteries exemptions;

(b) any loss relating to land where income from the land would not qualify for exemption;

(c) any miscellaneous loss not arising as a result of charitable activities;

(d) expenditure not incurred for charitable purposes only and not required to be taken into account in calculating the profits of a trade or property business carried on by the charitable company or the profit or loss on any miscellaneous transaction carried on by such a company;

(e) the amount of the charitable company funds invested in an investment other than an approved charitable investment;

(f) loans made by the company in an accounting period which are neither investments nor approved charitable loans.'

Tainted donations

[15.11] The first paragraph is amended to read as follows.

'There are anti-avoidance provisions which remove entitlement to tax reliefs and counteract tax advantages where a person makes a relievable charitable donation which is a 'tainted donation' (see below, but broadly a donation linked to arrangements for the donor to obtain a financial advantage). The provisions apply equally to donations to community amateur sports clubs (see **76.2** VOLUNTARY ASSOCIATIONS).'

21

Construction Industry Scheme

Registration

[21.5] The fifth paragraph under the heading 'Registration' is amended to read as follows.

'An application by a company for registration under the scheme may be made online on form CIS305. See www.gov.uk/government/publications/construction-industry-scheme-company-registration-cis305. HMRC also produce extensive guidance for contractors and sub-contractors in booklet CIS340 (www.gov.uk/government/publ

ications/construction-industry-scheme-cis-340). Where an application for gross payment is refused (or gross payment registration cancelled), the sub-contractor has a right of appeal (see below).'

The final paragraph on page 563 is amended to read as follows.

'Numerous cases have reached the tax tribunals and courts concerning the granting or withdrawal of gross payment status. The case of *Westview Rail Ltd* (TC00215) [2009] UKFTT 269 (TC) tested whether there were grounds for an appeal against cancellation of gross payment status. *Enderby Properties Ltd* (TC00396) [2010] UKFTT 85 (TC) and *GC Ware Electrics* (TC00499) [2010] UKFTT 197 tested whether insufficient funds constituted a reasonable excuse for late payments. *Grosvenor* (TC00227) [2009] UKFTT 283 (TC), *Ductaire Fabrications Ltd* (TC00288) [2009] UKFTT 350 (TC), *Pollard* (TC00563) [2010] UKFTT 269 (TC) and *Burns (t/a TK Fabrications)* (TC00371) [2010] UKFTT 58 (TC) are further examples of cases where HMRC cancelled gross payment status.

The financial consequences of cancellation of gross payment registration are not a relevant factor to be taken into account by HMRC when deciding how to exercise their discretion to cancel registration (*HMRC v J P Whitter (Waterwell Engineers) Ltd* CA 2016, [2017] STC 149).'

25

Creative Industries Reliefs

Introduction to creative industries reliefs

[25.1] A new paragraph is added at the end to read as follows.

'**Museums and galleries**

Legislation will be included in the Finance Bill 2017 to introduce tax relief for incorporated museums, galleries and other heritage institutions from 1 April 2017, following the existing creative industries reliefs. Relief will take the form of an additional deduction from taxable profits, or a repayable credit if the deduction results in a loss. The rates of relief will be set at 25% for touring exhibitions and 20% for permanent exhibitions, capped at £500,000 of qualifying expenditure per exhibition.

See www.gov.uk/government/publications/museums-and-galleries-tax-relief.'

26

Derivative contracts

Introduction to derivative contracts

[26.1] A new paragraph is added immediately before the Simon's Taxes reference at the end.

'Interest rate hedging products redress payments

HMRC have published guidance on the tax treatment of compensation payments made by certain banks as redress for the mis-selling of interest rate hedging products. Where the swap was taken out for the purposes of the company's trade, the redress payment should be treated as a trading receipt. See www.gov.uk/government/publications/tax-interest-rate-hedging-products-irhp.'

The credits or debits for an accounting period arising from a derivative contract

[26.7] A new paragraph is added at the end of the section headed 'Accounting periods beginning before 1 January 2016' as follows.

'In *Union Castle Mail Steamship Co Ltd v HMRC* FTT, [2016] SFTD 1057, a debit arising from the derecognition of a financial asset was disallowed on the grounds that there was no loss incurred by the company.'

27

Disclosure of Tax Avoidance Schemes

Introduction to disclosure of tax avoidance schemes

[27.1] The fourth paragraph is amended to read as follows.

'For HMRC guidance on the disclosure regime see www.gov.uk/govern ment/publications/disclosure-of-tax-avoidance-schemes-guidance.'

The last two paragraphs are replaced with the following.

'As announced in the Autumn Statement 2016, the government will consult on a requirement for businesses that create or promote complex offshore financial structures to notify HMRC of their creation and related client lists. The requirement will be targeted at structures which represent a higher risk of being used for evading UK taxes.

The consultation document can be found at www.gov.uk/government/ consultation s/tackling-offshore-tax-evasion-a-requirement-to-notify-hmrc-of-offshore-struc tures.'

28

Distributions

Items which are not distributions

[28.16] The list at the beginning of the section is amended to read as follows.

(a)   Distributions made in respect of share capital on winding up (see 77 WINDING UP). [*CTA 2010, s 1030*].

(b)   Distributions made in respect of share capital in anticipation of dissolution under *Companies Act 2006, s 1000 or 1003*. The maximum distributions are £25,000, otherwise all the distributed profits will be distributions. Further conditions apply. [*CTA 2010, s 1030A*].

(c)   A distribution as part of a merger to which *TCGA 1992, s 140E or 140F* applies (cross-border mergers) where the company ceases to exist as a result of the merger without being wound up, is treated as a distribution in respect of share capital in a winding up. [*CTA 2010, s 1031*].

(d)   Small distributions to members on dissolution of an unincorporated association which is of a social or recreational nature and has not carried on a trade or investment business. (HMRC Extra-Statutory Concession, C15).

(e)   Payments for group relief (or for the surrender of ACT on dividends paid prior to 6 April 1999) (see **34.16** GROUP RELIEF), except in so far as they exceed the amount surrendered. [*CTA 2010, s 183*].

(f)   *Share or loan interest* paid by registered societies within **23.1** CO-OPERATIVE AND COMMUNITY BENEFIT SOCIETIES (previously registered industrial and provident societies) or certain co-operative associations. [*CTA 2010, s 1055*].

(g)   *Dividends or bonuses* deductible in computing the income of registered societies within **23.1** CO-OPERATIVE AND COMMUNITY BENEFIT SOCIETIES (previously registered industrial and provident societies) or MUTUAL COMPANIES (**54**). [*CTA 2010, s 1056*].

(h)   *Dividends or interest* payable in respect of shares in, deposits with, or loans to, BUILDING SOCIETIES (**9**). [*CTA 2010, s 1054*]. However, this exemption does not apply with effect from 1 March 2013 to core capital deferred shares. [*SI 2013 No 460, Reg 3*].

(i)   *Stock dividends* (see Tolley's Income Tax under Savings and Investment Income). [*CTA 2010, ss 1049–1053*].
   For this purpose, a stock dividend is either one issued in lieu of cash, or a bonus issue of shares in respect of shares of a 'qualifying class'. In both cases, the issuing company must be UK-resident. In the case of bonus shares, shares are of a 'qualifying class' if shares of that class carry the right to bonus shares of that or another class under the terms of original issue or those terms as subsequently amended. There are special rules for the situation where bonus share capital (as defined) is converted into or exchanged for shares of a different class. 'Bonus share capital' means the share capital or part of it not issued for new consideration.
   There is provision for returns to be made to HMRC where stock dividends or bonus issues are made and rules for determining the return periods.

(j)   *Interest on securities* not within **28.5–27.7** above i.e. interest etc. paid in respect of certain securities, provided the securities are 'special securities', both companies are within the charge to corporation tax and the terms are commercial. However, this exemption does not apply to securities falling within the exceptions outlined at **28.8** above, for securities within CTA 2010, Sch 2 para 107. [*CTA 2010, s 1032*].

(k)   Money provided by a close company for the purchase of its shares by trustees of its profit sharing scheme. (CCAB Memorandum TR 308, June 1978).

(l)   Certain *purchases by a company of its own shares* (see **61** PURCHASE BY A COMPANY OF ITS OWN SHARES). [*CTA 2010, ss 1033–1047*].

(m)   Any 'relevant alternative finance' return within *CTA 2009, ss 507 or 513* is not treated as a distribution for corporation tax purposes. (See **4.7** ALTERNATIVE FINANCE ARRANGEMENTS.) [*CTA 2009, ss 507, 513*].

(n)   The transfer of a building society's business to a company. [*FA 1998, Sch 12 para 6*].

(o)   Interest and share dividends paid by a UK agricultural or fishing co-operative. [*CTA 2009, s 1057*].

(p)   A payment made on or after 26 October 2012 and in an accounting period ending before 1 January 2014 in respect of securities (other than shares) issued by a bank or the 'parent undertaking' of a bank that form part of the 'tier two capital resources' of the bank or parent undertaking. This provision does not apply, however, if there are arrangements a main purpose of which is to obtain a tax advantage for any person as a result of its application. 'Parent undertaking' is defined in *Financial Services and Markets Act 2000, s 420*, and '*tier two capital resources*' is as defined by the PRA Handbook (or, before 1 April 2013, the FSA Handbook of Rules and Guidance). [*CTA 2010, s 1032A; FA 2013, s 43(4)–(6); SI 2013 No 3209*].

(q)   With regard to expenditure incurred on or after 1 April 2013, the surrender to another group member of an amount in respect of an above the line R&D expenditure credit (see **63** RESEARCH AND DEVELOPMENT EXPENDITURE). [*CTA 2009, ss 104O, 104R; FA 2013, Sch 15*].

(r)   A payment in respect of a regulatory capital security, from 1 January 2014, which is a security that qualifies, or has qualified, as an Additional Tier 1 or Tier 2 instrument and forms, or formed, part of Additional Tier 1 or of Tier 2 capital for the purposes of Commission Regulation 575/2013 (which imposes prudential requirements on financial institutions). Anti-avoidance provisions apply if there are arrangements in place the main purpose, or one of the main purposes, of which is to obtain a tax advantage (within *CTA 2010, s 1139*) as a result of the application of this provision, such that the payment would not benefit from the exemption from being a distribution. Transitional rules apply with regard to such securities issued before 1 January 2014. For accounting periods commencing on or after 1 January 2016 the definition of regulatory capital security under these provisions is extended to include insurers' Tier 1 and Tier 2 compliant Solvency II instruments (within Commission Delegated Regulation (EU) 2015/35) issued in the form of debt. Transitional rules apply. [*SI 2013 No 3209, Reg 5; SI 2015 No 2056*].

30

Double Tax Relief

Mixing and onshore pooling

[30.11] The paragraph before the Simon's Taxes reference at the end is amended to read as follows.

'In *Peninsular & Oriental Steam Navigation Company v HMRC* CA, [2016] STC 2001 the CA held that a scheme devised to enhance double tax relief artificially by manipulating dividend payments to increase the amount of underlying tax did not work (without the need to consider recharacterisation under the *Ramsay* principle — see **5.2** ANTI-AVOIDANCE).'

Agreements in force

[30.16] This section is amended to read as follows.

'A list is given below of the double tax agreements made by the UK which are currently operative. The agreements have effect to the extent, and as from the operative dates, specified therein (SI numbers in round brackets). Additional notes for certain agreements are given after the list, together with details of agreements made but not yet in force.

Albania (2013/3145), **Antigua and Barbuda** (1947/2865; 1968/1096), **Argentina** (1997/1777), **Armenia** (2011/2722), **Australia** (1968/305; 1980/707; 2003/3199), **Austria** (1970/1947; 1979/117; 1994/768; 2010/2688), **Azerbaijan** (1995/762),

Bahrain (2012/3075), **Bangladesh** (1980/708), **Barbados** (2012/3076), **Belarus** (1995/2706 — see notes below), **Belgium** (1987/2053; 2010/2979), **Belize** (1947/2866; 1968/573; 1973/2097), **Bolivia** (1995/2707), **Bosnia-Herzegovina** (see note below), **Botswana** (2006/1925), **British Virgin Islands** (2009/3013), **Brunei** (1950/1977; 1968/306; 1973/2098; 2013/3146), **Bulgaria** (2015/1891; 1987/2054), **Burma** (see Myanmar below),

Canada (1980/709; 1980/1528; 1985/1996; 2003/2619; 2014/3274; 2015/2011), **Cayman Islands** (2010/2973), **Chile** (2003/3200), **China** (2011/2724; 2013/3142), **Croatia** (2015/2011), **Cyprus** (1975/425; 1980/1529), **Czech Republic** (see note below),

Denmark (1980/1960; 1991/2877; 1996/3165),

Egypt (1980/1091), **Estonia** (1994/3207), **Ethiopia** (2011/2725),

Falkland Islands (1997/2985), **Faroe Islands** (2007/3469; 1961/579; 1971/717; 1975/2190 until 6 April 1997), **Fiji** (1976/1342), **Finland** (1970/153; 1980/710; 1985/1997; 1991/2878; 1996/3166), **France** (2009/226),

Gambia (1980/1963), **Georgia** (2004/3325; 2010/2972), **Germany** (2010/2975; 1967/25; 1971/874; 2014/1874), **Ghana** (1993/1800), **Greece** (1954/142), **Grenada** (1949/361; 1968/1867), **Guernsey** (1952/1215; 1994/3209; 2015/2008; 2016/750), **Guyana** (1992/3207),

Hong Kong (2010/2974), **Hungary** (2011/2726),

Iceland (2014/1879; 1991/2879), **India** (1981/1120; 1993/1801; 2013/3147), **Indonesia** (1994/769), **Ireland** (1976/2151; 1976/2152; 1995/764; 1998/3151), **Isle of Man** (1955/1205; 1991/2880; 1994/3208; 2009/228; 2013/3148; 2016/749), **Israel** (1963/616; 1971/391), **Italy** (1990/2590), **Ivory Coast** (1987/169),

Jamaica (1973/1329), **Japan** (2006/1924; 2014/1881), **Jersey** (1952/1216; 1994/3210; 2015/2009; 2016/752), **Jordan** (2001/3924),

Kazakhstan (1994/3211; 1998/2567), **Kenya** (1977/1299), **Kiribati** (as per Tuvalu), **Korea, Republic of (South)** (1996/3168), **Kosovo** (2015/2007), **Kuwait** (1999/2036),

Latvia (1996/3167), **Lesotho** (1997/2986), **Libya** (2010/243), **Liechtenstein** (2012/3077), **Lithuania** (2001/3925; 2002/2847), **Luxembourg** (1968/1100; 1980/567; 1984/364; 2010/237),

Macedonia (2007/2127), **Malawi** (1956/619; 1964/1401; 1968/1101; 1979/302), **Malaysia** (1997/2987; 2010/2971), **Malta** (1995/763), **Mauritius** (1981/1121; 1987/467; 2003/2620; 2011/2442), **Mexico** (1994/3212; 2010/2686), **Moldova** (2008/1795), **Mongolia** (1996/2598), **Montserrat** (1947/2869; 1968/576; 2011/1083), **Morocco** (1991/2881), **Myanmar** (1952/751),

Namibia (1962/2352; 1962/2788; 1967/1490), **Netherlands** (2009/227; 1980/1961; 1983/1902; 1990/2152; 2013/3143), **New Zealand** (1984/365; 2004/1274; 2008/1793), **Nigeria** (1987/2057), **Norway** (2013/3144; 1985/1998; 2000/3247),

Oman (1998/2568; 2010/2687),

Pakistan (1987/2058), **Panama** (2013/3149), **Papua New Guinea** (1991/2882), **Philippines** (1978/184), **Poland** (2006/3323), **Portugal** (1969/599),

Qatar (2010/241; 2011/1684),

Romania (1977/57), **Russia** (1994/3213),

Saudi Arabia (2008/1770), **St. Christopher (St. Kitts) and Nevis** (1947/2872), **Serbia and Montenegro** (see note below), **Sierra Leone** (1947/2873; 1968/1104), **Singapore** (1997/2988; 2010/2685; 2012/3078), **Slovak Republic (Slovakia)** (see note below), **Slovenia** (2008/1796), **Solomon Islands** (1950/748; 1968/574; 1974/1270), **South Africa** (1969/864; 2002/3138; 2011/2441), **Spain** (2013/3152), **Sri Lanka** (1980/713), **Sudan** (1977/1719), **Swaziland** (1969/380), **Sweden** (2015/1891; 1984/366), **Switzerland** (1978/1408; 1982/714; 1994/3215; 2007/3465; 2010/2689),

Taiwan (2002/3137), **Tajikistan** (2014/3275), **Thailand** (1981/1546), **Trinidad and Tobago** (1983/1903), **Tunisia** (1984/133), **Turkey** (1988/932), **Tuvalu** (1950/750; 1968/309; 1974/1271),

Uganda (1952/1213; 1993/1802), **Ukraine** (1993/1803), **U.S.A.** (1980/568; 2002/2848), **USSR** (see note below), **Uzbekistan** (1994/770),

Venezuela (1996/2599), **Vietnam** (1994/3216),

Yugoslavia (1981/1815 and see note below),

Zambia (2014/1876; 1972/1721; 1981/1816), **Zimbabwe** (1982/1842).

Shipping & Air Transport only—Algeria (Air Transport only) (1984/362), Brazil (1968/572), Cameroon (Air Transport only) (1982/1841), Ethiopia (Air Transport only) (1977/1297 — now replaced by comprehensive agreement above), Hong Kong (Air Transport) (1998/2566), Hong Kong (Shipping Transport) (2000/3248), Iran (Air Transport only) (1960/2419), Jordan (1979/300), Lebanon (1964/278), Saudi Arabia (Air Transport only) (1994/767), Zaire (1977/1298).

Czechoslovakia

The Agreement published as *SI 1991 No 2876* between the UK and Czechoslovakia is treated as remaining in force between the UK and, respectively, the Czech Republic and the Slovak Republic. (HMRC Statement of Practice 5/93).

USSR

The Agreement published as *SI 1986 No 224* (which also continued in force the Air Transport agreement published as *SI 1974 No 1269*) between the UK and the former Soviet Union was to be applied by the UK as if it were still in force between the UK and the former Soviet Republics until such time as new agreements took effect with particular countries. It later came to light that Armenia, Georgia, Kyrgyzstan, Lithuania and Moldova did not consider themselves bound by the UK/USSR convention and were not operating it in relation to UK residents. Accordingly, the UK ceased to apply it to residents of those countries from 1 April 2002 for corporation tax and from 6 April 2002 for income tax and capital gains tax. (The

Agreement published as *SI 2001 No 3925* between the UK and Lithuania has effect from those dates.) A similar discovery has subsequently been made in relation to Tajikistan and the agreement ceased to be applied by the UK from 1 April 2014 for corporation tax and from 6 April 2014 for income tax and capital gains tax (see above for the current agreement with Tajikistan). The position for other former Republics (Belarus and Turkmenistan) with which new conventions are not yet in force remains as before (but see below for the agreements signed with both countries). (HMRC Statement of Practice 4/01 (replacing SP 3/92) and Revenue Tax Bulletin June 2001 p 864).

Yugoslavia

The Agreement published as *SI 1981 No 1815* between the UK and Yugoslavia is regarded as remaining in force between the UK and, respectively, Bosnia-Herzegovina, and Serbia and Montenegro (and, prior to the implementation of new agreements, Croatia, Slovenia and Macedonia). (HMRC Statements of Practice 3/04, 3/07).

Copies of double tax agreements and other statutory instruments published from 1987 onwards are available on the Stationery Office website at www.hmso.gov.uk/stat.htm.

Agreements not yet in force the agreement with Belarus had not yet entered into force in August 2008 and was then considered unlikely to enter into force in the near future. (HMRC Double Taxation Relief Manual DT3300). A protocol to the agreement with Belgium was signed on 14 March 2014 (see *SI 2014 No 1875*). A comprehensive agreement with Algeria was signed on 18 February 2015 (see *SI 2015 No 1888*). A comprehensive agreement with Senegal was signed on 26 February 2015 (see *SI 2015 No 1892*). A comprehensive agreement with Uruguay was signed on 24 February 2016 (see *SI 2016 No 753* — applies in the UK from 1 April 2017 for corporation tax purposes and from 6 April 2017 for capital gains tax purposes). A comprehensive agreement with the United Arab Emirates was signed on 12 April 2016 (see *SI 2016 No 754* — applies in the UK from 1 April 2017 for corporation tax purposes and from 6 April 2017 for capital gains tax purposes). A comprehensive agreement with Turkmenistan was signed on 10 June 2016 (see *SI 2016 No 1217* — applies in the UK from 1 April 2017 for corporation tax purposes and from 6 April 2017 for capital gains tax purposes). A comprehensive agreement with Colombia was signed on 2 November 2016. A new comprehensive agreement with Lesotho was signed on 3 November 2016.'

34

Group Relief

Arrangements for transfer of company to another group or consortium

[34.14] The text is amended to read as follows.

'Relief is denied where two companies are members of a group and 'arrangements' are in existence by virtue of which one company could leave the group and join another group, or any person could gain control of one company but not the other, or a third company could succeed to the trade of one of the companies.

Similar restrictions apply to consortium relief (see **34.19** below). There are also provisions to cover the situation where there are arrangements under which the consortium-owned company could leave the group or where the company could come under the control of a third company.

[*CTA 2010, ss 154, 155; FA 2013, s 31(2)*].

Definition of 'arrangements'

'*Arrangements*' for this purpose are those of any kind, whether in writing or not. The following, however, are not arrangements:

- the power of a Minister of the Crown, the Scottish Ministers or a Northern Ireland department to direct a statutory body as to the disposal of its (or any subsidiary's) assets; and
- for accounting periods ending on or after 1 April 2013, a condition imposed by, or agreed with a Minster of the Crown, the Scottish Ministers or a Northern Ireland department or a statutory body.

For accounting periods ending on or after 1 April 2013, a '*statutory body*' is specifically defined to mean a body (other than a company within the meaning of *Companies Act 2006, s 1(1)*) established by or under a statutory provision for the purposes of carrying out functions conferred on it by or under a statutory provision. The Treasury may, by order, specify that a particular body is or is not to be treated as a statutory body for this purpose.

[*CTA 2010, s 156(2); FA 2013, s 31(1)(4)*].

Arrangements which are in existence during the relevant period are within the definition irrespective of when they came into existence (*Pilkington Bros Ltd v CIR* (1982) 55 TC 705, HL) and without regard to the extent of their implementation (*Irving v Tesco Stores (Holdings) Ltd* (1982) 58 TC 1, HL).

Arrangements which could not legally be carried out without variation of the underlying agreement were ineffective for these purposes (*Scottish and Universal Newspapers Ltd v Fisher* [1996] STC (SCD) 311).

The appointment of a receiver constitutes arrangements for these purposes (*Farnborough Airport Properties Co Ltd v HMRC* FTT, [2016] SFTD 826).

The restriction of relief applies only to accounting periods or parts thereof during which the arrangements subsisted (*Shepherd v Law Land plc* (1990) 63 TC 692, HL).

Exception for joint venture companies

Agreements between the companies holding shares or securities in a joint venture company, which allow or require remaining members to acquire the holding of a departing company (and which allow or require a departing company to transfer its shares to remaining members) are not regarded as arrangements (or option arrangements — see **34.4** above) for the purposes of the above provisions until one of the following specified events occurs:

(a) the voluntary departure of a member;
(b) the commencement of liquidation, administration or receivership of a member;
(c) a serious deterioration in the financial condition of a member;
(d) a change in the control or ownership of a member;

(e) a default by a member in performing its obligations under the terms of an agreement between the members or with the joint venture company, including its articles of association;

(f) an external change in the commercial circumstances in which the undertaking operates such that its viability is seriously threatened;

(g) unresolved disagreement among the members;

(h) any contingency of a similar kind provided against, but not intended to happen, when the agreement in question was entered into.

A provision in the articles of a joint venture company providing for the suspension of a member's voting rights on the occurrence of a specified event is not regarded as bringing arrangements into existence until the specified event actually occurs. These provisions do not apply if the persons who would acquire shares, securities or control of the joint venture company in consequence of the occurrence of a specified event could (alone or with connected persons) dictate the timing of the acquisition in advance of the specified event. The definition of 'connected persons' in CTA 2010, s 1122 applies for this purpose, but persons are not regarded as connected solely by virtue of their interest in the joint venture company.

[*CTA 2010, ss 155A, 174A*].

Exception for mortgage of securities

If shares or securities in a company are used as security for a mortgage, the mortgage is not in itself regarded as constituting arrangements (or options arrangements) until a default or other event occurs which enables the mortgagee to exercise his rights against the mortgagor (unless the default is remedied before the mortgagee exercises his rights). [*CTA 2010, s 155B, 174B*].

Exceptions under SP 3/93

'Arrangements' (and 'option arrangements') are the subject of an HMRC Statement of Practice. The special rules relating to 'arrangements' are not applied to the following cases:

(I) Straightforward negotiations for the disposal of shares or securities in a company, before the point at which an offer is accepted subject to contract or on a similar conditional basis.

(II) An offer to the public at large of shares in a business, unless there are exceptional features.

(III) Operations leading towards the disposal of shares or securities in a company, until any necessary approval by shareholders has been given, or the company's directors become aware that it will be given.

(IV) Where, following negotiations with a number of potential purchasers, the vendor concentrates on one, unless there were an understanding between them in the character of an option, e.g. if the offer, whether or not formally made, were allowed to remain open for an appreciable period, allowing the potential purchaser to choose the moment to create a bargain.

(V) Company reconstructions requiring the approval of shareholders, until the necessary approval is given or the directors are aware that it will be given.

"Arrangements" (but not "option arrangements") may exist even though not enforceable. If an agreement provides for the creation of specified option rights exerciseable at some future time, 'option arrangements' come into existence when the agreement is entered into.

(HMRC Statement of Practice, SP 3/93).

See also HMRC Company Taxation Manual, CTM80175–CTM80205.

Simon's Taxes. See D2.251, D2.252.'

35

Groups of Companies — Financing Costs and Income

Introduction to groups of companies — financing costs and income

[35.1] The following paragraph is added at the end.

'Future developments

Legislation is to be introduced in the Finance Bill 2017 so that, from 1 April 2017, interest and other finance expenses that can be offset against profits of large multinational enterprises will be limited to 30% of a group's taxable earnings. This measure will be accompanied by the introduction of a group ratio rule, an exemption for public benefit infrastructure and a £2 million de minimis threshold. The existing debt cap legislation will be replaced with a modified debt cap, to ensure the net UK interest deduction does not exceed the total net interest expense of the worldwide group. Amounts of restricted interest can be carried forward indefinitely, whereas any unused interest allowance may only be carried forward for up to five years.

See www.gov.uk/government/publications/corporation-tax-tax-deductibility-of-corporate-interest-expense.'

36

HMRC — Administration

International co-operation

[36.13] The first paragraph is amended to read as follows:

'Further to global moves to combat fraud and tax evasion the UK has entered into international agreements for mutual assistance in tax enforcement, covering exchange of information foreseeably relevant to the administration, enforcement or recovery of UK or foreign tax, the recovery of debts and the service of documents relating to UK or foreign tax. *FA 2006, ss 173–175* make certain provisions in respect of such arrangements. Many of these information exchange agreements are based on the 2002 OECD model — a list of such agreements can be found at www.gov.uk/government/collections/tax-information-exchange-agreements.'

The penultimate sentence in the third paragraph under the heading 'Automatic information exchange with the USA and others' is deleted.

The text under the heading 'Implementing regulations' is amended to read as follows.

'The *International Tax Compliance Regulations 2015 (SI 2015 No 878)* came into force on 15 April 2015 (with effect from that date for FATCA, and from 1 January 2016 otherwise), and implement the provisions of the updated Administrative Co-operation Directive, the multilateral CAA (with regard to the CRS), and the agreement to implement FATCA.

With effect from 30 September 2016, financial institutions (and persons providing advice or services to individuals relating to offshore accounts, income or services) must inform certain clients of information that HMRC will receive under the regulations. Institutions must identify the clients affected and notify them on or before 31 August 2017.

[*SI 2015 No 878; SI 2015 No 1839; SI 2016 No 899*].

With regard to the IGAs signed with the Crown Dependencies and various overseas territories, see for example, the *International Tax Compliance (Crown Dependencies and Gibraltar) Regulations 2014 (SI 2014 No 520).*

For further details of the FATCA IGA between the US and the UK see: www.gov.uk/government/publications/uk-us-automatic-exchange-of-information-a greement/uk-us-automatic-exchange-of-information-agreement.'

Assets Recovery

[36.14] The text is amended to read as follows.

'See also **58.8** PAYMENT OF TAX.

The National Crime Agency is an independent government agency and not part of HMRC. Its remit is to use criminal confiscation, civil recovery and taxation functions to recover money and assets that have come from criminal activity, thus depriving criminals of the proceeds of their crime. There are provisions in *Proceeds of Crime Act 2002 (Pt 6)* in respect of certain serious crimes that allow the functions of HMRC to be undertaken by the NCA.

The powers were originally given to the Asset Recovery Agency. This Agency was subsequently merged with the Serious Organised Crime Agency, which in turn became part of the National Crime Agency in 2013.

In order to carry out HMRC functions, the agency must have reasonable grounds to suspect that:

(a)   income arising or a gain accruing to a person in respect of a chargeable period is chargeable to income tax or is a chargeable gain and arises or accrues as a result (whether wholly or partly, directly or indirectly) of the 'criminal conduct' of that person or another; or

(b)   a company is chargeable to corporation tax on its profits arising in a chargeable period and the profits arise as a result (whether wholly or partly, directly or indirectly) of the criminal conduct of the company or another person,

and must serve a notice on HMRC specifying the person or company, the period or periods concerned, and the functions which they intend to carry out. The periods involved may include periods beginning before the *Act* was passed.

Where the agency is acting in such a capacity it is immaterial that a source cannot be identified for any income. Thus an assessment made by the agency under *TMA 1970, s 29* (discovery assessment) in respect of income charged to tax under *ITTOIA 2005, Pt 5 Ch 8* (income not otherwise charged — see Tolley's Income Tax under Miscellaneous Income) cannot be reduced or quashed only because it does not specify (to any extent) the source of the income.

The agency may cease carrying out the functions specified in the notice (originally served on HMRC) at any time, but *must* so cease where the conditions allowing the original notice to be made are no longer satisfied. Any assessment made under *TMA 1970, s 29* is subsequently invalid to the extent that it does not specify a source for income.

For the above purposes, *'criminal conduct'* is conduct which constitutes an offence anywhere in the UK or which would do so if it occurred there, but does not include conduct constituting an offence relating to a matter under the care and management of HMRC.

It should be noted that the vesting of a function in the agency under these provisions does not divest HMRC or its officers of their functions (so that, for example, HMRC can continue to carry out routine work). Certain functions, as listed in *Proceeds of Crime Act 2002, s 323(3)*, cannot be carried out by the agency. For example, if the agency serves notice in relation to a company and in respect of a chargeable period or periods, the general HMRC functions vested in the agency do not include functions relating to any requirement which is imposed on the company in its capacity as an employer and relates to a tax year which does not fall wholly within the chargeable period(s).

In respect of actions carried out by the agency in the exercise of HMRC functions taxpayers have the same rights of appeal as any other taxpayer, thus appeals may be made to the appropriate tribunal. In hearing such appeals, the tribunal may be assisted by one or more assessors selected for their special knowledge and experience of the matter to which the appeal relates from a panel appointed for the purpose by the Lord Chancellor.

[*Proceeds of Crime Act 2002, ss 317, 318(1)(2), 319, 320(1)–(3), 323(1)(3), 326(1)(2); SI 2003 No 120; ITTOIA 2005, Sch 1 para 582*].

A company whose tax affairs are being investigated by the agency should check its website (www.nationalcrimeagency.gov.uk) for guidance on how their cases will be dealt with.

See **7.3** ASSESSMENTS for a case involving a discovery assessment raised by the National Crime Agency.

HMRC officers undertaking criminal investigations into direct tax or tax credits offences have powers to seize suspected criminal cash under the *Proceeds of Crime Act 2002* and to exercise search and seizure warrants under that Act.

[*FA 2013, s 224; SI 2016 No 208*].'

37

HMRC Extra-Statutory Concessions

[37.2] The first paragraph is amended to read as follows.

'The following is a summary of the concessions applicable to companies published by HMRC. The published list of ESCs can be found at www.gov.uk/government /collections/extra-statutory-concessions.'

The final paragraph on page 1102 'C9 Associated close and small companies' is deleted.

The first paragraph on page 1103 'C10 Groups of companies: arrangements' and the fifth paragraph on that page 'C16 Dissolution of companies under *Companies Act 1985, ss 652, 652A:* are deleted.

38

HMRC Investigatory Powers

Information and documents

[38.4] The fourth paragraph is amended to read as follows.

'Documents must be produced for inspection either: at a place agreed to by the recipient of the notice and an HMRC officer; or at a place (other than one used solely as a dwelling) that an HMRC officer reasonably specifies. HMRC may specify in the notice that documents should be sent to them by post or email (*TeING Ltd v HMRC* UT, [2016] UKUT 363 (TCC), 2016 STI 2545).'

Data-gathering powers

[38.12] The following paragraph is added immediately before the heading 'Penalties' but after the list of statutory references at the end.

'Money service businesses (i.e. businesses that provide money transfer, cheque cashing and currency exchange services) are to be added to the list of data-holders in summer 2017. See www.gov.uk/government/publications/data-from-money -service-businesses.'

HMRC's practice in cases of serious tax fraud

[38.18] The fourth paragraph under the heading 'Contractual disclosure facility' is amended to read as follows.

'If a taxpayer wishes to own up to a fraud without waiting to be contacted by HMRC, he may complete form CDF1 (www.gov.uk/government/publications/volu ntary-disclosure-contractual-disclosure-facility-cdf1); HMRC will then consider the taxpayer for a CDF contract. Alternatively, disclosures, whether under the CDF, one of HMRC's targeted campaigns, or otherwise, may be made online using the digital disclosure service at www.gov.uk/government/publications/hm-revenue-and-custom s-disclosure-service. See www.gov.uk/government/publications/hmrc-your-guide-to-making-a-disclosure for HMRC guidance on voluntary disclosures.'

41

Income Tax in Relation to a Company

Payments by a company etc

[41.2] The second paragraph after list item (b) on page 1152 is amended to read as follows.

'In *Ardmore Construction Ltd and Colin Perrin v HMRC* [2015] UKUT 633 (TCC), the Upper Tribunal confirmed that the First-tier Tribunal was correct in its two earlier decisions (*Perrin v HMRC* [2014] UKFTT 223 (TC) and *Ardmore Construction Ltd v HMRC* [2014] UKFTT 453 (TC)) to take a 'multi-factorial' approach to determining whether interest arose from a source in the UK for the purposes of *ITA 2007, s 874(1)*. The lower tribunal has been correct to give weight to the residence of the debtor, which was in the UK, and to the substantive source of the payments for the interest, in preference to the place of residence or activity of the creditor.

Statutory interest payable to creditors from the surplus arising in the administration of a company is not yearly interest (*Lomas v HMRC* Ch D, [2016] EWHC 2492 (Ch), 2016 STI 2782).'

43

Interest on Overdue Tax

Interest rates

[43.5] The text is replaced with the following.

'The interest rate is determined by criteria contained in Treasury regulations made by statutory instrument; see *SI 1989 No 1297, Regs 3ZAA, 3ZB*.

It is understood that a denominator of 366 is used in calculations of such interest regardless of whether or not a leap year is involved.'

Self-assessment

[43.6] This section is amended to read as follows.

'Overdue corporation tax payments

For underpayments of corporation tax for accounting periods ending on or after 1 July 1999, the following rates of interest apply.

- **2.75% p.a. from 23 August 2016**
- 3.00% p.a. from 29 September 2009 to 22 August 2016
- 2.50% p.a. from 24 March 2009 to 28 September 2009
- 3.50% p.a. from 27 January 2009 to 23 March 2009
- 4.50% p.a. from 6 January 2009 to 26 January 2009
- 5.50% p.a. from 6 December 2008 to 5 January 2009
- 6.50% p.a. from 6 November 2008 to 5 December 2008
- 7.50% p.a. from 6 January 2008 to 5 November 2008
- 8.50% p.a. from 6 August 2007 to 5 January 2008
- 7.50% p.a. from 6 September 2006 to 5 August 2007
- 6.50% p.a. from 6 September 2005 to 5 September 2006
- 7.50% p.a. from 6 September 2004 to 5 September 2005
- 6.50% p.a. from 6 December 2003 to 5 September 2004
- 5.50% p.a. from 6 August 2003 to 5 December 2003
- 6.50% p.a. from 6 November 2001 to 5 August 2003
- 7.50% p.a. from 6 May 2001 to 5 November 2001
- 8.50% p.a. from 6 February 2000 to 5 May 2001
- 7.50% p.a. from 6 March 1999 to 5 February 2000
- 8.50% p.a. from 7 January 1999 to 5 March 1999

Overdue instalment payments

For accounting periods ending on or after 1 July 1999, a special rate of interest applies in the case of certain 'large' companies, which are required to make instalment payments in respect of their corporation tax liabilities (see **58.3** PAYMENT OF TAX). The special rate of interest applies to any unpaid instalments until nine months after the end of the accounting period (whereafter the normal interest rate (above) applies). Details are as follows.

- **1.25% p.a. from 15 August 2016**
- 1.50% p.a. from 16 March 2009 to 14 August 2016
- 2.00% p.a. from 16 February 2009 to 15 March 2009
- 2.50% p.a. from 19 January 2009 to 15 February 2009
- 3.00% p.a. from 15 December 2008 to 18 January 2009
- 4.00% p.a. from 17 November 2008 to 14 December 2008
- 5.50% p.a. from 20 October 2008 to 16 November 2008
- 6.00% p.a. from 21 April 2008 to 19 October 2008
- 6.25% p.a. from 18 February 2008 to 20 April 2008
- 6.50% p.a. from 17 December 2007 to 17 February 2008
- 6.75% p.a. from 16 July 2007 to 16 December 2007
- 6.50% p.a. from 21 May 2007 to 15 July 2007
- 6.25% p.a. from 22 January 2007 to 20 May 2007
- 6.00% p.a. from 20 November 2006 to 21 January 2007
- 5.75% p.a. from 14 August 2006 to 19 November 2006
- 5.50% p.a. from 15 August 2005 to 13 August 2006
- 5.75% p.a. from 16 August 2004 to 14 August 2005
- 5.50% p.a. from 21 June 2004 to 15 August 2004
- 5.25% p.a. from 17 May 2004 to 20 June 2004
- 5.00% p.a. from 16 February 2004 to 16 May 2004
- 4.75% p.a. from 17 November 2003 to 15 February 2004
- 4.50% p.a. from 21 July 2003 to 16 November 2003
- 4.75% p.a. from 17 February 2003 to 20 July 2003
- 5.00% p.a. from 19 November 2001 to 16 February 2003
- 5.50% p.a. from 15 October 2001 to 18 November 2001
- 5.75% p.a. from 1 October 2001 to 14 October 2001
- 6.00% p.a. from 13 August 2001 to 30 September 2001

- 6.25% p.a. from 21 May 2001 to 12 August 2001
- 6.50% p.a. from 16 April 2001 to 20 May 2001
- 6.75% p.a. from 19 February 2001 to 15 April 2001
- 7.00% p.a. from 20 April 2000 to 18 February 2001
- 8.00% p.a. from 21 February 2000 to 19 April 2000
- 7.75% p.a. from 24 January 2000 to 20 February 2000
- 7.50% p.a. from 15 November 1999 to 23 January 2000
- 7.25% p.a. from 20 September 1999 to 14 November 1999
- 7.00% p.a. from 21 June 1999 to 19 September 1999
- 7.25% p.a. from 19 April 1999 to 20 June 1999
- 7.50% p.a. from 15 February 1999 to 18 April 1999
- 8.00% p.a. from 18 January 1999 to 14 February 1999
- 8.25% p.a. from 7 January 1999 to 17 January 1999

[*SI 1989 No 1297, Regs 3ZA, 3ZB; SI 1998 No 3175, Reg 7; SI 1998 No 3176, Regs 4–6; SI 2000 No 893*].'

45

Investment Companies and Investment Business

Receipts

[45.7] The text is replaced by the following:

'Industrial development grants

A grant received by a company with investment business under *Industrial Development Act 1982, s 7* or *8* (or Northern Ireland equivalent) is an amount to which the charge to corporation tax on income applies.

This rule does not apply if the grant is designated as made towards specified capital expenditure or as compensation for the loss of capital assets, or if the grant is for all or part of a corporation tax liability (including one already paid). It also does not apply if the grant is taken into account in calculating corporation tax profits under another provision.

[*CTA 2009, s 1252*].

Contributions to local enterprise organisations or urban regeneration companies — disqualifying benefits

If a management expenses deduction has been made by a company under **45.4**(viii) above and the company or a connected person receives a 'disqualifying benefit' which is attributable in any way to the contribution, the company is treated as receiving an amount equal to the value of the benefit and to which the charge to corporation tax on income applies.

For this purpose, 'disqualifying benefit' has the same meaning as at **45.4**(viii) above. So far as the value of a benefit is taken into account in determining the amount of the original deduction it is excluded from this provision.

[*CTA 2009, s 1253*].

Repayments under Financial Services and Markets Act 2000

A payment made to a company with an investment business, as a result of a repayment provision made either under *Financial Services and Markets Act 2000, s 136(7)* or *s 214(1)* or by scheme rules (i.e. the rules referred to in *Financial Services and Markets Act 2000, Sch 17 para 14(1)*) for fees to be refunded in certain cases, is treated as an amount to which the charge to corporation tax on income applies. Payments treated as trading or property business receipts are ignored for this purpose.

[*CTA 2009, s 1254*].

Simon's Taxes. See D7.301.'

46

Investment Funds

Unauthorised unit trusts

[46.22] The first paragraph is amended to read as follows.

'Special provisions apply to the income and gains of a unit trust scheme not within **46.3** above (an 'unauthorised unit trust' (UUT)), the trustees of which are UK resident. Such a trust is outside the rules in **46.5** above (tax treatment of AIFs).'

The text under the heading '6 April 2014 onwards' down to the heading 'Exempt UUTs' is replaced with the following.

'The current tax treatment of the trustees and unit holders of UUTs applies with effect on and after 6 April 2014, subject to the transitional rules below. There are separate provisions for approved exempt and non-exempt UUTs and their investors.'

49

Leasing

Changes to Lease Accounting Standards

[49.2] The fourth paragraph is deleted.

The words 'per *s 53(3)*' are deleted from the fifth paragraph.

A new paragraph is added at the end but immediately before the Simon's Taxes reference to read as follows.

'In January 2016, the IASB published IFRS 16 on accounting for leases which sets out the principles of recognition, measurement, presentation and disclosure of leases for both lessee and lessor. A fundamental change from the previous treatment under IAS 17 is that for lessees the distinction is removed between finance leases and operating leases. The above provisions apply such that for tax purposes the amounts relating to leases will continue to be determined by reference to the old accounting standards. However, HMRC issued a consultation document on 9 August 2016 on options for changes to the tax rules on leases of plant and machinery to take account of the change to IFRS 16. See www.gov.uk/government/consultations/lease-accounting-changes.'

50

Loan Relationships

Taxation of loan relationships

[50.2] The penultimate paragraph on page 1378 is amended to read as follows.

'In *Stagecoach Group plc v HMRC* FTT, [2016] SFTD 982 it was held that debits claimed by the taxpayer related to a recapitalisation scheme using forward subscription agreements, which were not loan relationships, and therefore no debits were allowable.'

Recognition of profit — generally accepted accounting practice

[50.8] The first sentence of the paragraph immediately before the heading 'Amortised cost accounting treatment' is amended to read as follows.

'For cases in which the Tribunal ruled on whether a particular way of accounting was compliant with the relevant accounting standards see *Greene King plc v HMRC* CA, [2016] EWCA Civ 782, 2016 STI 2441 and *Fidex Ltd v HMRC* CA, [2016] STC 1920. In *Cater Allen International Ltd v HMRC* FTT, [2015] UKFTT 232 (TC) the Tribunal considered the interest coupon under a repo and held that the accounting treatment was paramount.'

Change of accounting practice

[50.15] The list of statutory references immediately before the heading 'Change in accounting policy where loan relationship as permanent-as-equity' is amended to read as follows.

'[CTA 2009, ss 315–318, 465B, Sch 2, para 62; F(No 2)A 2015, Sch 7, paras 10, 11, 52; SI 2004 Nos 3271, 3347; SI 2014, No 3187; SI 2014, No 3325; SI 2016 No 1234].'

Credits and debits relating to capital expenditure

[50.75] The last paragraph is amended to read as follows.

'In *Stagecoach Group plc v HMRC* FTT, [2016] SFTD 982, a debit in respect of forward subscription agreements made under a scheme for the recapitalisation of two group companies was held not to fall within the above provisions.'

51

Losses

Introduction to losses

[51.1] The final two paragraphs are replaced with the following.

'In *English Holdings v HMRC* FTT, [2016] UKFTT 436 (TC), [2016] STI 2549 a non-UK resident company was able to set off against its trading profits subject to income tax a loss incurred in a trade which, if profitable, would have been subject to corporation tax. (For the charge to corporation tax and income tax on non-resident companies generally see **64.5** RESIDENCE.)

For commentary on devolution of the power to set the corporation tax rate in Northern Ireland to the Stormont Assembly and consequential modification of the treatment of losses, see **1.1** INTRODUCTION: CHARGE TO TAX, RATES AND PROFIT COMPUTATIONS.

The Government intends to make changes to the rules governing the carry forward of losses so that losses arising on or after 1 April 2017 will, when carried forward, be able to be offset against profits from different types of income and other group companies. Where a company or group's profit is above £5 million, the losses carried forward will only be able to be offset against up to 50% of the profits over £5 million. Carried forward losses arising at any time will be subject to this restriction.

Draft legislation published in December 2016 also contains provisions which prevent loss buying. Where a company or group is acquired, any losses arising after 1 April 2017 but before the acquisition, will not be available to the purchaser group for five years. A targeted anti-avoidance rule will also be enacted to prevent abuse of the reforms to loss relief. A consultation response document was published on 5 December 2016 (see www.gov.uk/government/consultations/reforms-to-corporati on-tax-loss-relief-consultation-on-delivery).

See www.gov.uk/government/publications/corporation-tax-reform-of-loss-relief.'

Company reconstructions — common ownership

[51.10] A new case reference is added at the end of the second paragraph on page 1489 as follows.

'See *HMRC v Leekes Ltd*, UT [2016] STC 1970.'

55

Offshore Funds

Introduction to offshore funds

[55.1] The following text is added at the end.

'The Government announced at Autumn Statement 2016 that secondary legislation will be introduced to alter the calculation of reportable income from offshore funds. This will affect the measure of income on which UK investors pay tax and will apply for reporting periods commencing on or after 1 April 2017. Draft regulations have been published for comment by 27 January 2017 (see www.gov.uk/government/up loads/system/uploads/attachment_data/file/574558/4014_Offshore_Funds_Regs_ v.1.pdf).

Broadly, the change ensures that performance fees incurred by offshore reporting funds are not deductible when calculating UK investors' reportable income. Such expenses will instead reduce investors' taxable gains when they dispose of their holdings in an offshore reporting fund.

See www.gov.uk/government/publications/offshore-funds-calculation-of-reportable -income/offshore-funds-calculation-of-reportable-income.'

Computing reportable income

[55.4] The list at beginning of page 1552 is amended to read as follows.

'Adjustments to the income statement are required for:

*   capital items and (for reporting periods beginning on or after 1 April 2017) miscellaneous items;
*   special classes of income e.g. group income from wholly-owned subsidiaries, income from other reporting funds, income from certain non-reporting funds, interest income computed in an unacceptable way;
*   equalisation arrangements operated by the fund when a participator disposes of an interest in it (see below);
*   wholly-owned subsidiaries (95% or 100% subsidiaries — see further below), the receipts, expenditure, assets and liabilities of which are attributed to the fund;
*   Interests in other offshore funds — where a reporting fund (A) invests in another reporting fund (B) then the excess of income reported by B over what was distributed by B to A must be added to fund A's reportable income; where the investment is in a non-reporting fund then (if certain conditions are met) the fund undertakes its own calculation of the income from the non-reporting fund and includes this in its reportable income. From 27 May 2011 the addition is made in the period of account in which B's fund distribution date falls, or if earlier, the period of account in which the reported income from B in respect of that reporting period is recognised in A's accounts. From 27 May 2011 the fund distribution date is the date six months following the last day of the reporting period. Before 27 May 2011 it was the date on which the report was issued to participants where this was issued within six months of the end of the reporting period, otherwise the last day of the reporting period.'

The list of statutory references immediately before the Simon's Taxes reference on page 1553 is amended to read as follows.

'[*SI 2009 No 3001, Regs 59–72, 94; SI 2011 No 1211, Regs 33, 34, 40; SI 2017 No 240*].'

56

Partnerships

Introduction to partnerships

[56.1] The text is amended to read as follows.

'Companies can form partnerships with individuals, other companies and trustees. Persons carrying on a trade in partnership are referred to collectively as a '*firm*'. A '*company partnership*' is a partnership in which at least one partner is a company. A company member of a partnership is liable to pay corporation tax on its profits.

This chapter looks at the tax treatment of companies in partnership. Further guidance can be found in HMRC's Company Tax Manual at CTM36505ff. The legislation is contained in the main in *CTA 2009, Pt 17*. [*CTA 2009, s 1257*].

HMRC issued a consultation document on 9 August 2016 on proposed changes to the tax treatment of partnerships. The main proposals are:

* to treat a person as a member of a partnership for tax purposes if they are notified to HMRC as partners;
* where a business structure includes partnerships as partners, to provide that those responsible for paying the tax on a share in the partnership profit are treated as partners in the first partnership for tax purposes;
* to explore options to protect the exchequer where details of partners entitled to trading or property business partnership profits are not provided by the partnership;
* to introduce legislation to confirm that the profit-sharing arrangements as set out in the partnership agreement are the determining factor in identifying the partners' profit shares;
* to introduce legislation to provide that the basis of allocation of tax-adjusted profit should be the same as the allocation of the accounting profit or loss between the partners; and
* to introduce legislation to provide that the profits of company partners liable to income tax will be calculated as if a non-UK resident company were carrying on the business.

See further www.gov.uk/government/consultations/partnership-taxation-proposals-t o -clarify-tax-treatment.'

57

Patent Income

Introduction to patent income

[57.1] The final paragraph is replaced with the following.

'For HMRC guidance, see the Corporate Intangibles Research and Development Manual CIRD200000 onwards.

Legislation will be introduced in Finance Bill 2017 to ensure that where R&D is undertaken collaboratively by two or more companies under a 'cost sharing arrangement' (CSA), the companies involved will be treated neutrally as a result of structuring their affairs in this way. The rules will apply from 1 April 2017.

Essentially, the new rules will ensure that where a company acquires an interest in a CSA, the consideration paid will count as an acquisition cost for the purpose of calculating the R&D fraction. Similarly, where a company disposes of an interest in a CSA, an appropriate amount of any consideration received will be treated as IP income.

See www.gov.uk/government/publications/corporation-tax-patent-box-cost-sharing -arrangements/corporation-tax-patent-box-cost-sharing-arrangements.'

Relevant IP profits — company not new entrant, new qualifying IP rights for accounting periods beginning before 1 July 2021

[57.7] The sixth paragraph is amended to read as follows.

'The conditions in (ii) and (iii) above operate by reference to 2 January 2016 rather than 1 July 2016 where the person who assigned the right or granted the licence is not within the charge to corporation tax or a designated foreign tax, the person and the company are connected and a main purpose of the assignment or grant was the avoidance of a foreign tax. For the list of designated foreign taxes see *SI 2016 No 1181*.'

59

Penalties

In the Contents list at the start of the chapter, the second item under 'Miscellaneous' is amended to read as follows.

'Reasonable excuse for failure 59.25'

Introduction to penalties

[59.1] The following point is added after item '22' at the end of the table on page 1656.

'23. Enabling off-shore tax evasion FA 21016, s 162, Sch 20	Higher of 100% of the potential lost revenue and £3,000. If the original tax non-compliance resulted in a penalty under *FA 2015, Sch 21* (offshore asset moves), higher of 50% of the potential lost revenue in respect of the original tax non-compliance and £3,000.	59.21'

The first paragraph after the table on page 1656 is deleted.

The following text is added at the end.

'Enablers of tax avoidance

Following consultation conducted earlier in 2016, a new penalty will be introduced in Finance Bill 2017. The penalty will apply to individuals or entities ('enablers') who enable the use of abusive tax arrangements which HMRC later defeat. It will apply only to steps taken by enablers after Royal Assent to Finance Bill 2017.

The definition of 'enabler' will distinguish between those who design, market or otherwise facilitate avoidance arrangements and those who just advise, report or otherwise provide an opinion on such arrangements and whose advice does not result in any changes to the arrangements. Anyone unwittingly becoming involved in arrangements will be excluded.

Arrangements will be treated as abusive if they meet a 'double reasonableness test'. This will ensure that the penalty does not inhibit genuine commercial transactions. External scrutiny will be provided by the GAAR Advisory Panel.

The penalty will apply to arrangements relating to income tax, corporation tax, CGT, petroleum revenue tax, diverted profits tax, apprenticeship levy, inheritance tax, SDLT or annual tax on enveloped dwellings.

The amount of the penalty will be equal to the consideration received by the enabler for anything done to enable the arrangements. HMRC will be able to publish information about an enabler liable to penalties exceeding a specified amount (yet to be fixed).

See www.gov.uk/government/publications/strengthening-sanctions-and-deterrents-for-tax-avoidance.

Reasonable care

The circumstances in which a taxpayer is considered to have taken reasonable care for the purposes of the penalty provisions of *FA 2007, Sch 24* (see **52.8** below) are to be amended. The changes will apply to documents relating to tax periods which begin on or after 6 April 2017 and end on or after the date of Royal Assent to Finance Bill 2017.

Following the changes it will be presumed in cases of defeated avoidance that a person has been careless unless they can prove they have taken reasonable care. The legislation will explicitly describe circumstances and events which do not represent taking reasonable care. These will include:

(a)   advice addressed to a third party or without reference to the taxpayer's specific circumstances and use of the scheme;

    (b)   advice commissioned or funded by a party with a direct financial interest in selling the scheme or not provided by a disinterested party; and

    (c)   material produced by parties without the relevant tax or legal expertise or experience to advise on complicated avoidance arrangements (typically the sort of material used to market arrangements and not amounting to advice on the legal options necessary for a taxpayer to assess the likely success of the scheme or the risks).

See www.gov.uk/government/publications/strengthening-sanctions-and-deterrents-for-tax-avoidance.'

Enabling offshore tax evasion

[59.21] The first sentence of the first paragraph is amended to read as follows.

'With effect for acts or omissions occurring on or after 1 January 2017, a penalty is payable by a person (P) who has 'enabled' another person (Q) to carry out offshore tax evasion or non-compliance if:'

The list of statutory references in the second paragraph under the heading 'Double jeopardy' is amended to read as follows.

'[FA 2016, s 162, Sch 20 paras 1–9, 15; SI 2016 No 1249].'

60

Property Income

Charge to tax

[60.2] The text under the heading 'Annual Tax on Enveloped Dwellings' is amended to read as follows.

'Annual Tax on Enveloped Dwellings

For a detailed overview of the Annual Tax on Enveloped Dwellings please refer to:

Companies, partnerships with at least one company member and collective investment schemes (including unit trusts) who own residential dwellings situated in the UK are chargeable to an annual residential property tax, the Annual Tax on Enveloped Dwellings (ATED) if the value of the dwellings on relevant dates exceeds a specified threshold. The charge applies as from 1 April 2013 and is payable annually, with the chargeable period running for 12 months from 1 April each year. The value threshold, for chargeable periods beginning on or after 1 April 2016, is £500,000. For chargeable periods beginning on 1 April 2015 the threshold is £1 million; previously it was £2 million. Genuine property rental businesses and taxpayers holding properties for charitable purposes or properties run as a commercial business can claim a relief from the tax on an annual basis. The tax is administered by HMRC and requires those within the scope of the tax to make annual ATED returns.

See also www.gov.uk/guidance/annual-tax-on-enveloped-dwellings-the-basics and **Simon's Taxes** Division B6.7.

[*FA 2013, ss 94–174; FA 2014, ss 109, 110; FA 2015, ss 70, 73; FA 2016, ss 134–136; SI 2014 No 854*].'

Furnished holiday lettings

[60.7] The section is amended to read as follows.

'In so far as a property business consists in the 'commercial letting' of 'furnished holiday accommodation' (a 'furnished holiday lettings (FHL) business') for an accounting period, it is treated as a trade for the purposes of the carry forward of losses against profits of the same trade (see below).

In addition, a furnished holiday lettings business is a qualifying activity for the purposes of capital allowances on plant and machinery (see **11.4** CAPITAL ALLOWANCES ON PLANT AND MACHINERY).

In contrast to furnished lettings generally, it is possible to claim capital allowances on plant or machinery provided for use in a dwelling-house, but neither the replacement domestic items relief at **60.5** above nor its predecessor the 10% wear and tear allowance in **60.6** above can be claimed as an alternative.

All commercial lettings of furnished holiday accommodation by a particular company (or partnership) are treated as a single trade or, for capital allowances purposes, as a single qualifying activity, separate from any other trade or other qualifying activity carried on by that company. The same applies (though separately) to all such lettings outside the UK but in the EEA (see below).If a UK property business consists only partly of the commercial letting of furnished holiday accommodation, the profits and losses of the separate parts of the business must be separately calculated. If there is a letting of accommodation only part of which is holiday accommodation, such apportionments are to be made as —just and reasonable. The same rules apply to an overseas property business by reference to accommodation outside the UK but in the EEA (see below).

Relief for losses

An FHL business is treated as a trade for the purpose of loss relief under **51.5** LOSSES (carry-forward of losses against profits of the same trade in subsequent accounting periods). A UK business and an overseas business are treated separately for this purpose.

There is nothing to prevent losses of a UK property business (whether in the same accounting period or brought forward from earlier periods) from being set against profits of a UK FHL business as the latter is part of the UK property business. The same applies as regards losses of an overseas property business against profits of an EEA (excluding the UK) FHL business. However, losses of an FHL business cannot be set against profits of an ordinary rental business.

Property outside the UK

The special treatment of furnished holiday lettings described above applies also to the commercial letting of qualifying furnished holiday accommodation outside the UK but in the European Economic Area (EEA). It does not to apply to furnished holiday accommodation outside the EEA. The EEA consists of: Austria, Belgium, Bulgaria, Cyprus, Czech Republic, Denmark, Estonia, Finland, France, Germany, Gibraltar, Greece, Hungary, Iceland, Ireland, Italy, Latvia, Liechtenstein, Lithuania, Luxembourg, Malta, Netherlands, Norway, Poland, Portugal, Romania, Slovakia, Slovenia, Spain, Sweden, Switzerland and the UK.

Meaning of 'commercial letting'

Commercial letting is letting (whether or not under a lease) on a commercial basis and with a view to the realisation of profits. For a case in which the 'commercial letting' test was satisfied despite a significant excess of interest over letting income, see *Walls v Livesey* (Sp C 4), [1995] SSCD 12, but see also *Brown v Richardson* (Sp C 129), [1997] SSCD 233 in which the opposite conclusion was reached. See Revenue Tax Bulletin October 1997 pp 472, 473 for HMRC's view of the requirements in this respect.

Meaning of 'furnished holiday accommodation'

For any tax year, *'holiday accommodation'* is accommodation which:

(a)   is available for commercial letting to the public generally as holiday accommodation for at least 210 days in the 12-month period referred to below; and

(b)   is so let for at least 105 such days (but see below as regards the possibility of averaging).

See also the 'period of grace' rule described below.

Any period of more than 31 consecutive days during which the accommodation is in the same occupation (otherwise than because of abnormal circumstances) does not count towards fulfilling the number of days required in (b) above. Any such period is known as a *'period of longer-term occupation'*, and if, during the 12-month period referred to below, more than 155 days fall during periods of longer-term occupation, the accommodation is not *'holiday accommodation'*.

The 12-month period referred to above is the 12 months ending with the last day of the accounting period in question, unless:

(1)   the accommodation was not let by the person concerned as furnished accommodation in the 12 months immediately preceding the accounting period, in which case the 12-month period runs from the date such letting commenced in the accounting period in question; or

(2)   the accommodation was let by the person concerned as furnished accommodation in the 12 months immediately preceding the accounting period but is not so let in the 12 months immediately after the accounting period, in which case the 12-month period is the 12 months ending with the date such letting ceased in the accounting period in question.

Holiday accommodation is *'furnished holiday accommodation'* if the tenant is entitled to use of the furniture.

Averaging

In satisfying the test in (b) above, averaging may be applied to the number of let days of any or all of the accommodation let by the same company which either is holiday accommodation or would be holiday accommodation if it satisfied the test on its own. An election for averaging must be made within two years beginning at the end of the accounting period to which it is to apply. It must specify the accommodation to be included in the averaging calculation. Holiday accommodation cannot be included in more than one averaging election for an accounting period. See below for an example of how averaging works.

An averaging election has to be made separately for properties in the UK and for properties in the EEA. A single election cannot cover both.

Period of grace

A period of grace is allowed if:

- during an accounting period (Period 1), a company lets furnished holiday accommodation that qualifies for the special treatment (whether on its own or as a result of averaging but other than as a result of this 'period of grace' rule);
- it continues to let the accommodation during the following accounting period (Period 2) or the following two accounting periods (Periods Years 2 and 3);
- it does not qualify for the special treatment for Period 2 (or Periods 2 and 3) purely because the letting condition in (b) above is not met; and
- there was a genuine intention to meet that letting condition for Period 2 (or for each of Periods 2 and 3).

If the company so elects for either Period 2 or each of Periods 2 and 3, the accommodation is treated as qualifying for the special treatment for the accounting period or periods in question. Holiday accommodation that qualifies for the special treatment by virtue only of this rule cannot be included in an averaging claim. If an election is not made for Period 2, no election can be made for Period 3. Any election must be made within two years beginning at the end of the accounting period to which it is to apply.

[CTA 2009, ss 264–269A; CTA 2010, ss 65, 67A; FA 2016, ss 73(7), 74(3)].

[CTA 2009, ss 264–269, Sch 1 paras 171, 172; CAA 2001, ss 15–17; ITTOIA 2005, Sch 1 paras 526–528; CTA 2009, Sch 1 paras 476, 477].

See Tolley's Capital Gains Tax as regards relief from capital gains tax in respect of furnished holiday lettings.

Simon's Taxes. See B6.401–B6.405, B9.110.

Example

X Ltd owns and lets out furnished holiday cottages. None is ever let to the same person for more than 31 consecutive days. Three cottages have been owned for many years but Rose Cottage was acquired on 1 April 2016 (and first let on that day) while Ivy Cottage was sold on 30 April 2016 (and last let on that day).

In B Ltd's accounting period ending 31 December 2016, days available for letting and days let are as follows.

	Days available	Days let
Honeysuckle Cottage	230	160
Primrose Cottage	150	110
Bluebell Cottage	215	90
Rose Cottage	220	70
Ivy Cottage	60	15

Additional information

Rose Cottage was let for 40 days between 1 January 2017 and 31 March 2017.

Ivy Cottage was let for 60 days in the period 1 May 2015 to 31 December 2015 but was available for letting for 160 days in that period.

Qualification as 'furnished holiday accommodation'

Honeysuckle Cottage qualifies as it meets both the 210-day availability test and the 105-day letting test.

Primrose Cottage does *not* qualify although it is let for more than 105 days as it fails to satisfy the 210-day test. Averaging (see below) is only possible where it is the 105-day test which is not satisfied.

Bluebell Cottage does not qualify by itself as it fails the 105-day test. However it may be included in an averaging election.

Rose Cottage qualifies as furnished holiday accommodation. It was acquired on 1 April 2016 so qualification in the accounting period ending 31 December 2016 is determined by reference to the period of 12 months beginning on the day it was first let, in which it was let for a total of 110 days.

Ivy Cottage was sold on 30 April 2016 so qualification is determined by reference to the period from 1 May 2015 to 30 April 2016 (the last day of letting). It does not qualify by itself as it was let for only 75 days in this period but it may be included in an averaging election.

Averaging election for accounting period ending 31 December 2016

	Days let
Honeysuckle Cottage	160
Bluebell Cottage	90
Rose Cottage	110
Ivy Cottage	75

$$\frac{160 + 90 + 110 + 75}{4} = 108.75 \text{ days}$$

All four cottages included in the averaging election now qualify as furnished holiday accommodation as each is deemed to have been let for 108.75 days in the accounting period ending 31 December 2016.

If the average had been less than 105, the two cottages which qualify in any case could have been included in an averaging election together with one of the non-qualifying cottages (leaving the other as non-qualifying). If averaging three cottages still did not improve the position, an average of just two could be tried.

See **60.6** for position where a furnished holiday business is carried on and there is also another property business or transaction.'

64

Residence

Non-resident companies

[64.5] The first paragraph is amended to read as follows.

'A non-UK resident company is liable to corporation tax if it carries on a trade of dealing in or developing UK land (see **72.2** TRANSACTIONS IN UK LAND) or if it carries on any other trade in the UK through a 'permanent establishment' there. See further

64.6 below for the profits of permanent establishments in respect of which non-resident companies are liable to tax and for the liability of 'UK representatives'.'

The charge to income tax

[64.7] The following text is added after the first paragraph.

'The government announced at the Autumn Statement 2016 that it will consult after Budget 2017 on the case and options for bringing taxable income received by non-resident companies into the UK corporation tax regime. The policy objective is to ensure that resident and non-resident companies are treated equally in the general framework of corporation tax.

See www.gov.uk/government/publications/finance-bill-2017-draft-legislation-overvi ew-documents/overview-of-legislation-in-draft para 2.9.

In *English Holdings v HMRC* FTT 2016, [2017] SFTD 20, a non-UK resident company carried on a trade in the UK through a permanent establishment (so that the profits would be chargeable to corporation tax) and also carried on a UK property business (the profits of which were chargeable to income tax). The First-tier Tribunal held that the company could set off losses from the UK trade against profits from the UK property business under *ITA 2007, s 64*.'

65

Returns

Enquiries into returns

[65.16] The table after the first paragraph under the heading 'Conduct of enquiry' is amended to read as follows.

'COP 8	Specialist investigations (fraud and bespoke avoidance) (August 2014).
COP 9 (2014)	HMRC investigations where we suspect tax fraud (June 2014).
CC/FS1a	General information about compliance checks (November 2014).
CC/FS1b	General information about checks by Campaigns and Projects (January 2017).
CC/FS1c	General information about compliance checks into large businesses (September 2012).
CC/FS2	Compliance checks — information notices (May 2015).
CC/FS3	Compliance checks — visits by agreement or with advance notice (October 2015).
CC/FS4	Compliance checks — visits — unannounced (March 2009).
CC/FS5	Compliance checks — visits — unannounced — tribunal approved (March 2009).

CC/FS6	Compliance checks — what happens when we find something wrong (March 2009).
CC/FS7a	Compliance checks series — penalties for inaccuracies in returns or documents (December 2016).
CC/FS7b	Compliance checks series — penalties for not telling us about an under-assessment (September 2012).
CC/FS9	Compliance checks — Human Rights Act and penalties (October 2015).
CC/FS10	Compliance checks — suspending penalties for careless inaccuracies in returns or documents (December 2016).
CC/FS11	Compliance checks — penalties for failure to notify (December 2016).
CC/FS13	Compliance checks — publishing details of deliberate defaulters (April 2010).
CC/FS14	Compliance checks — managing serious defaulters (October 2015).
CC/FS15	Compliance checks — self assessment and old penalty rules (October 2015).
CC/FS17	Compliance checks — higher penalties for income tax and CGT involving offshore matters (October 2015).
CC/FS18(a)	Compliance checks — late filing penalties (October 2015)
CC/FS21	Compliance checks — alternative dispute resolution (October 2015)
CC/FS22	Compliance checks — sending electronic records to HMRC (October 2015)
CC/FS23	Compliance checks — third party information notices (May 2015)
CC/FS24	Tax avoidance schemes — accelerated payments (January 2017)
CC/FS30a	Tax avoidance schemes — penalties for follower notices (October 2016)
CC/FS34	Compliance checks — general anti-abuse rule and provisional counteraction notices (December 2016)
CC/FS38	Compliance checks — serial tax avoidance — warning notices (October 2016)'

Completion of enquiry

[65.19] The fifth paragraph on page 1868 is amended to read as follows.

'An application for judicial review of a closure notice was unsuccessful in *R (oao Archer) v HMRC* QB, [2017] EWHC 296 (Admin), 2017 STI 328. The notice did not state the tax dues and was therefore defective. However, the taxpayer should have challenged the notice by making an appeal. If an appeal had been made the Tribunal would have cured the defect in the notice by applying *TMA 1970, s 114(1)* (see **7.2** ASSESSMENTS).'

The following text is added after the Simon's Taxes reference at the end of the page 1868.

'The Finance Bill 2017 will include legislation to enable HMRC and taxpayers to conclude discrete matters in an enquiry where more than one issue is open. This will be done by issuing a new partial closure notice (PCN) ahead of the final closure of an enquiry. HMRC will be able to issue a PCN either in agreement with the taxpayer, at their own discretion, or when directed to do so by the First-tier Tax Tribunal on application by a taxpayer.

HMRC will use the new power in cases where there is tax avoidance, high complexity, or where a large amount of tax is at risk. Where HMRC issue a partial closure notice and amend a person's tax return, the taxpayer will have a right to appeal and ask for payment of the tax to be postponed. Tax repayments arising from a PCN need not automatically be repaid, e.g. where tax is due in respect of other issues not covered by the PCN.

The legislation will come into effect from Royal Assent to the Finance Bill 2017 and will apply both to enquiries open at that time, and to future enquiries.

For details, see www.gov.uk/government/publications/tax-enquiries-closure-rules.'

66

Small Profits — Reduced Rates

Associated companies

[66.4] The text under the heading Meaning of 'control' is amended to read as follows.

"*Control*' is as defined in *CTA 2010, ss 450, 451*, see **17.6** CLOSE COMPANIES. That definition is, however, modified as follows.

(a) Fixed rate preference shares (as defined) held by a company are ignored in determining if one company is under the control of another if the company holding the shares is not a close company, takes no part in the management or conduct of the issuing company or of its business, and subscribed for the shares in the ordinary course of a business which includes the provision of finance.
[*CTA 2010, s 28*].

(b) A company is not under the control of another company if the only connection (past or present) between the two is that one company is a loan creditor (within *CTA 2010, s 453*) of the other and either the creditor company is not a close company or the creditor relationship arose in the ordinary course of the creditor company's business. Likewise, where two companies are controlled by the same person which is a loan creditor of each company, that person's rights as loan creditor are ignored in determining whether the two companies are associated. There must be no other connection (past or present) between the two companies, and the loan creditor must either not be a close company or the creditor relationship with each company must arise in the ordinary course of the creditor's business.
[*CTA 2010, s 29*].

(c) Where two companies are controlled by the same person by virtue of rights or powers held in trust by that person, those rights or powers are ignored in determining whether the two companies are associated, where there is no other connection (past or present) between the two companies. [*CTA 2010, s 30*].

(d) HMRC will not attribute the rights and duties of associates (as within *CTA, s 451* ('control': rights to be attributed)) in determining whether two companies are associated, or not, when the relationship between the two companies is not one of substantial commercial interdependence.

Regulations set out which factors should be taken into account to determine 'substantial commercial interdependence'. These provide that when establishing such interdependence the degree to which companies are financially, economically or organisationally interdependent should be taken into account.

[*CTA 2010, s 27; SI 2011 No 1784*].

See HMRC Company Taxation Manual CTM03770 onwards for HMRC's views on substantial commercial interdependence, including a number of examples of situations in which companies are (or are not) financially, economically and organisationally interdependent. Two companies will be treated as financially interdependent if, in particular, one gives financial support (directly or indirectly) to the other or each has a financial interest in the affairs of the same business. Two companies will be treated as economically interdependent if, in particular, the companies seek to realise the same economic objective, the activities of one benefit the other, or the companies have common customers. Two companies will be treated as organisationally interdependent if, in particular, the businesses of the companies have to use common management, common employees, common premises or common equipment.

See HMRC Company Taxation Manual, CTM60250 for HMRC's view of control where companies are under the control of more than one person or group of persons. For two companies to be under the control of the same persons, an irreducible group of persons having control of one must be identical with an irreducible group of persons having control of the other (i.e. in neither case could any definition of control be satisfied if any one of them were excluded).

In *Gascoines Group Ltd v Inspector of Taxes and related appeals* [2004] STC 844, a company controlled by trustees of a trust was considered to be associated with other companies controlled by the settlor of that trust. The trustees were associates of the settlor by virtue of what is now *CTA 2010, s 448(1)(b)* and therefore, the rights of the trustees were to be attributed to the settlor who was to be taken to have control over the company controlled by the trustees.

In *Seascope Insurance Services Ltd v HMRC* [2011] UKFTT 828 (10 January 2012) the company (S) was a wholly-owned subsidiary of a UK company, which in turn was owned by a company (G) which was resident in Liberia. S claimed marginal relief, on the basis that it had two associated companies. HMRC rejected the claim, on the basis that S had not provided sufficient information about its Liberian parent G (and possible overseas associated companies). The First Tier Tribunal found for the taxpayer — although the burden of proof falls on the taxpayer, the standard of proof is the balance of probabilities. S had provided sufficient information to show on the balance of probabilities that it had no more associated companies.

In *Ghelanis Superstore & Cash & Carry Ltd v HMRC* FTT, [2014] SFTD 835 a company (G) claimed small profits relief. HMRC rejected the claim on the basis that G had an associated company (E). The First-tier Tribunal dismissed G's appeal, finding that the issued capital of G and E was owned by the same seven family members, albeit in slightly different ratios, and that three of those seven had a 'controlling combination' in both companies.'

The section 'Information powers' on page 1889 is deleted.

68

Time Limits

Film tax, television, video games and theatrical production relief

[68.14] The first paragraph is amended to read as follows.

'A claim for film tax relief, for television, video games or theatrical production tax relief or for orchestra tax relief must be made in a company tax return (or amended return) for the accounting period for which the claim is made, within one year of the filing date for that return or by such later time as HMRC may allow. It can similarly only be amended or withdrawn by amendment of the company tax return within the same time limit. See 25 CREATIVE INDUSTRIES RELIEFS. [FA 1998, Sch 18 para 83W].'

69

Trade Profits — Income and Specific Trades

Avoidance schemes

[69.4] The following is added as the penultimate paragraph.

'In *Investec Asset Finance plc v HMRC* FTT, [2016] SFTD 677, two financial dealing companies acquired interests in partnerships as part of a scheme to avoid being taxed on lease rental income. Both companies were held to be carrying on two trades, one being their sole financial trades and the other being their share of the partnership profits treated as the profits of a separate trade. The costs of purchasing the partnership interests and making further contributions to the partnerships were deductible revenue expenses in the sole trades.'

Patents

[69.49] The second paragraph on page 1956 is amended to read as follows.

'See also 56 PATENT INCOME for the 'Patent Box' regime. This allows companies to elect to apply a 10% corporation tax rate (as phased in from 1 April 2013) to profits attributable to qualifying intellectual property, which includes patents granted by the UK Intellectual Property Office and the European Patent Office, as well as supplementary protection certificates, regulatory data protection and plant variety rights.'

The third paragraph on page 1956 which relates to the cross reference to '56 PATENT INCOME' is deleted.

Tonnage tax

[69.67] The last sentence of the fifth paragraph is deleted.

70

Trading Expenses and Deductions

In the Contents list at the start of the chapter, the sixth item under the heading 'Employees (and directors) — remuneration 70.26' which reads 'Disguised remuneration rules 70.32' is deleted.

Employee benefit contributions

[70.29] The text is amended to read as follows.

'There are statutory rules for the timing of deductions for 'employee benefit contributions' (EBCs). They apply instead of the more general rules at 70.28 above. For these purposes, an *'employee benefit contribution'* is made if, as a result of any act or omission, property is held, or may be used, under an 'employee benefit scheme' or there is an increase in the total net value of any such property. An *'employee benefit scheme'* is a trust, scheme or other arrangement for the benefit of persons who are, or include, present of former employees of the employer or persons linked with present or former employees. The definition is extended to also include, insofar as it would not otherwise come within the definition, a relevant arrangement under the income tax disguised remuneration provisions (i.e. a relevant arrangement within *ITEPA 2003, s 554A(1)(b)* to which *s 554A(1)(c)* applies) and any other arrangement connected (directly or indirectly) with that relevant arrangement. The question of whether a person is linked with another is determined as for the purposes of the disguised remuneration provisions (see *ITEPA 2003, s 554Z1*).

A deduction is allowed only to the extent that, during the period in question or within nine months after the end of it, 'qualifying benefits' are provided, or 'qualifying expenses' are paid, out of the contributions. (If the employer's contri-bution is itself a qualifying benefit, it is sufficient that the contribution be made during the period or within those ensuing nine months.) Any amount thus disallowed remains available for deduction in any subsequent period during which it is used to provide qualifying benefits. For these purposes, qualifying benefits are treated as provided, and expenses are treated as paid, as far as possible out of EBCs, with no account being taken of any other receipts or expenses of the scheme manager.

A *'qualifying benefit'* is a payment of money or transfer of assets (other than by way of loan) that:

(a)   gives rise to *both* a charge to income tax on employment income and a charge to NICs (or would do so but for available exemptions for duties performed outside the UK); or

(b)   is made in connection with termination of employment; or

(c)   is made under an employer-financed retirement benefits scheme.

However, a payment or transfer within (c) above is a qualifying benefit only if it gives rise to an income tax charge under *ITEPA 2003, Pt 6 Ch 2* or *Pt 9* or is an excluded benefit (within *ITEPA 2003, s 393B(3)*).

A 'chargeable relevant step' is also the provision of a qualifying benefit. A *'chargeable relevant step'* is a relevant step within the income tax disguised remuneration provisions which gives rise to a charge under *ITEPA 2003, Pt 7A Ch 2*.

'Qualifying expenses' are those expenses (if any) of the scheme manager in operating the scheme that would have been deductible in computing profits if incurred by the employer.

Money benefits are treated for the above purposes as provided at the time the money is treated as received for the purposes of income tax on employment income.

To the extent that the provision of a qualifying benefit is a chargeable relevant step (see above), the benefit is treated as provided when the relevant step is taken or, if later, when the employee begins his employment with the employer.

Where a qualifying benefit takes the form of the transfer of an asset which meets a condition at (a) to (c) above, the amount provided is the aggregate of:

(i)   the amount that would otherwise be deductible by the employer (in a case where the scheme manager acquired the asset from the employer);

(ii)   the amount expended on the asset by the scheme manager; and

(iii)   (in a case where the transfer is a chargeable relevant step and so far as not already taken into account under (i) or (ii)) the cost of the relevant step.

If, however, the amount charged to income tax under *ITEPA 2003* (or which would be so charged if the duties of employment were performed in the UK) is lower than that aggregate, any amount deductible under these provisions at any time is limited to that lower amount; this rule is aimed at a situation where the asset falls in value after its acquisition by the scheme manager but before its transfer to the employee (Treasury Explanatory Notes to the 2003 Finance Bill).

If the provision of a qualifying benefit is a chargeable relevant step which is not covered by the above and does not involve a sum of money, the amount provided is the cost of the relevant step. However, the amount provided cannot exceed the amount that is charged to tax under *ITEPA 2003* in relation to the relevant step or would be so charged if the employee had not been non-UK resident in any tax year. This limit applies equally if the chargeable relevant step does involve a sum of money.

These restrictions do not apply to disallow deductions for consideration given for goods or services provided in the course of a trade or profession or for contributions to a registered pension scheme, qualifying overseas pension scheme (if the employee is a relevant migrant member) or accident benefit scheme (as defined). They also do not apply to any deductions that are allowable under **70.33–70.38** below (employee share acquisitions), **70.39** below (share incentive plans) or **70.40** below (qualifying employee share ownership trusts).

Computations prepared before the end of the said nine-month period must be prepared by reference to the facts at the time of computation. If any contributions are used for qualifying purposes after that time, but within the nine months, the computation may be adjusted accordingly (subject to the normal time limits for amending company tax returns).

[*CTA 2009, ss 1290–1297, Sch 2 para 141; FA 2014, s 283, Sch 37 para 22*].

Payments to a trust the beneficiaries of which were members of employees' families were held to fall within these restrictions in *Sempra Metals Ltd v HMRC* (Sp C 698), [2008] SSCD 1062. If a contrived scheme is effected to achieve the opposite result to that intended by Parliament, it fails if only because for that very reason the contributions then have a duality of purpose (see **70.79** below) that itself undermines a deduction (*Scotts Atlantic Management Ltd v HMRC* UT, [2015] STC 1321).

Simon's Taxes. See **B2.422.**

Future developments

In relation to employee benefit contributions made, or to be made, on or after 1 April 2017 (for corporation tax purposes) legislation, to be included in Finance Bill 2017, will prevent companies claiming a deduction when computing their taxable profits for contributions to a disguised remuneration scheme unless PAYE income tax and NICs are paid within a specified period. The draft legislation builds on the restrictions already in force under *CTA 2009, s 1290* on deductions for employee benefit contributions, ie contributions made to create or enhance an employee benefit scheme. Under the new rules a company, when computing taxable profits for a period of account, will not be able to deduct a contribution to an employee benefit scheme unless any associated PAYE and NICs are paid within 12 months after the end of that period of account. Associated PAYE and NICs are those arising in respect of benefits which are provided out of, or by way of, the employee benefit contribution. It will also be specified that where a deduction would otherwise be allowable for an amount of employees' remuneration in respect of which employee benefit contributions are made (or are to be made), the deduction is to be treated as a deduction in respect of employee benefit contributions and not as a deduction in respect of remuneration, thus bringing it within the restrictions. There will also be a new time limit preventing any deduction of employee benefit contributions for a period of account beginning more than five years after the end of the period of account in which the contributions were made.

See www.gov.uk/government/publications/tackling-disguised-remuneration-update.'

Disguised remuneration rules

[70.32] This section is deleted.

72

Transactions in UK Land

Introduction to transactions in UK land

[72.1] The penultimate sentence in the fourth paragraph is amended to read as follows.

'In this connection, the UK's treaties with Guernsey, Jersey and the Isle of Man have been amended with backdated effect from 16 March 2016.'

The first paragraph on page 2086 is amended to read as follows.

'See also the HMRC guidance at www.gov.uk/government/publications/profits -from-a-trade-of-dealing-in-or-developing-uk-land-guidance.'

73

Transfer Pricing

Advance pricing agreements

[73.16] The penultimate paragraph on page 2123 is amended to read as follows.

'For a detailed explanation of how APAs are administered, see HMRC Statement of Practice, SP 2/10 and HMRC International Manual, INTM422000 onwards. The contact address for APA applications and other information is APA Team Leader, CTIS Business International, 11th Floor East, Euston Tower, 286 Euston Road, London NW1 3UH.'

76

Voluntary Associations

Introduction to voluntary associations

[76.1] The text paragraph is amended to read as follows.

'A club or society may be established as a company or as an unincorporated association of individuals. Whichever form it takes, it is liable to corporation tax on income (other than that generated from members e.g. membership fees or catering income from sales to members) and on capital gains. However, special rules apply to certain types of club, which in some cases offer a number of tax advantages.

This chapter covers the taxation treatment of certain commonly-found clubs and societies.'

Community amateur sports clubs

[76.2] The text is amended to read as follows.

'Certain tax exemptions can be claimed by sports clubs which are registered with HMRC as community amateur sports clubs ('*registered clubs*').

For a club to be eligible to register, it must, and its constitution must require it to:

- be 'open to the whole community';
- be 'organised on an amateur basis'; and
- have as its main purpose the provision of facilities for, and promotion of participation in, one or more 'eligible sports'.

The club must also meet the location condition, the management condition and the income condition.

For the above purposes, a club is '*open to the whole community*' if membership is open to all, and the club facilities are available to members, without discrimination (leaving aside necessary differentiation on grounds of age, gender or disability relative to a particular sport). Additionally, fees must be set at a level which does not pose a significant obstacle to membership, use of the facilities or full participation in club activities. Costs are deemed to represent a significant obstacle if the total of the membership fees and sporting activity costs exceed £520 per year and the club has not made arrangements to ensure that the costs do not represent an obstacle to membership. With effect from 1 April 2015, a club is not eligible to register if it receives membership fees exceeding £1,612 in respect of any member for any year. For the meaning of 'membership fees', 'sporting activity costs' and for the increase or decrease of the limits for periods of more than or less than a year see *SI 2015 No 725, Regs 7–9.*

A club is not prevented from being open to the whole community simply because it charges different fees for different descriptions of persons.

A club is '*organised on an amateur basis*' if it meets the following four conditions.

(a)   The club must be non-profit making, i.e. its constitution must require surplus income or gains to be reinvested in the club and must not permit the distribution of club assets (whether in cash or in kind) to members or third parties. However, donations by a club to charities or other registered clubs are allowed.

(b)   It must provide only the following benefits for members and their guests:

-    provision of sporting facilities and suitably qualified coaches;
-    reasonable provision and maintenance of club-owned sports equipment;
-    provision of, or reimbursement of the costs of, coaching courses;
-    provision of insurance cover and medical treatment;
-    reimbursement of reasonable and, with effect from 1 April 2015, necessary travel or subsistence expenses incurred by players, match officials and, with effect from 1 April 2015, coaches, first aiders and accompanying individuals travelling to away matches;
-    reasonable provision of post-match refreshments for players and match officials; and
-    sale or supply of food or drink as a social adjunct to the sporting purposes of the club.

(c)   It does not exceed the limit on paid players. The limit is, broadly, £10,000 per year. For the detailed rules see *SI 2015 No 725, Regs 11–13.*

(d)   The club's constitution must provide for any net assets on the dissolution of the club to be applied for the purposes of:

-    a charity;
-    another registered club; or
-    the governing body of an eligible sport for the purposes of which the club existed, for use in related community sport,

as approved by the members of the club in general meeting or by its governing body.

An '*eligible sport*' is one designated as such by Treasury order for the purposes of these provisions. See *SI 2002 No 1966* which designates for these purposes sports appearing on the National Sports Councils list of activities recognised by them.

A club is not regarded as a community amateur sports club if the number of social members within the club exceeds 50% of the total members. For these purposes a social member is defined as a member who either does not participate or only occasionally participates in the sports activities of the club. For the meaning of 'participation' and 'occasional participation' and for the method of calculating the percentage of social members see *SI 2015 No 725, Regs 16–19*.

A club meets the location condition if it is established in an EU member State or a territory specified in HMRC regulations and its facilities for eligible sports are all in one such State or territory. Iceland, Norway and (from 31 July 2014) Liechtenstein have been specified by regulations for these purposes.

A club meets the management condition if its managers are fit and proper persons. For this purpose, the managers are the persons with the general control and management of the administration of the club. If this condition is not met for a period of time it is nevertheless treated as met throughout that period if HMRC consider either that the failure has not prejudiced the purposes of the club or that it is just and reasonable for the condition to be treated as met. The expression 'fit and proper' is not defined and so takes its natural meaning. HMRC consider that the fit and proper person test is the same as that for charities (see **15.1** CHARITIES).

A club meets the income condition if the total of its trading receipts and property receipts does not exceed £100,000 for an accounting period. The limit is reduced proportionately where the accounting period is less than 12 months. The receipts taken into account are those that would be included in computing the club's trading income and property income for corporation tax if the exemptions for such income did not apply.

[*CTA 2010, ss 658(1)–(1C), 659–661CA; FA 2012, s 52; FA 2013, Sch 21; SI 2010 No 1904; SI 2014 No 1807; SI 2015 Nos 674, 725*].

For HMRC guidance on eligibility conditions see www.gov.uk/government/publica tions/community-amateur-sports-clubs-detailed-guidance-notes/community-amateu r-sports-clubs-detailed-guidance-notes.

Registration

Applications for registration are made to HMRC. Registration may be backdated (possibly to before the date of the application).

HMRC may terminate a club's registration (possibly with retrospective effect) if it appears to them that the club is not, or is no longer, entitled to be registered.

HMRC must notify a club of a decision to register it, to refuse its application or to terminate its registration. The club may appeal against any such decision by notice in writing to HMRC within 30 days of the date of the notification. The notice of appeal must specify the grounds of appeal. The provisions of *TMA 1970* relating to five APPEALS apply to such an appeal. If not dismissing the appeal, the Tribunal may either remit the matter to HMRC for reconsideration, or, as applicable, direct that the club be registered from a particular date, rescind a termination of registration, or direct that a termination take effect on a particular date.

HMRC publishes the names and addresses of registered clubs. This enables potential donors to confirm that they are donating to a registered club (and, therefore, that the donation may qualify for gift aid relief — see below). For a list of the names of registered clubs see www.gov.uk/government/publications/community-amateur-spo rts-clubs-casc-registered-with-hmrc--2.

[CTA 2010, ss 658(2)–(5), 670, 671].

Tax exemptions

Registered clubs enjoy a number of exemptions from tax.

UK trading income

A club that is a registered club throughout an accounting period can claim for its UK trading income for the period to be exempt from corporation tax if the following two conditions are met.

The first condition is that the receipts that would otherwise be brought into account in calculating the club's UK trading income for the period do not exceed £50,000. The threshold is proportionately reduced for periods of less than 12 months. For accounting periods beginning before 1 April 2015 the threshold was £30,000. Periods which straddle 1 April 2015 are treated as two separate accounting periods for the purpose of applying the limit and the receipts apportioned between them.

The second condition is that the whole of the UK trading income for the period is applied for 'qualifying purposes'. '*Qualifying purposes*' means purposes of providing facilities for, and promoting participation in, one or more eligible sports (and in the following paragraphs, '*non-qualifying purposes*' are to be construed accordingly).

[CTA 2010, ss 661(3), 662; FA 2013, Sch 21 para 6; SI 2014 No 3327].

UK property income

A club that is a registered club throughout an accounting period may make a claim for its UK property income to be exempt from corporation tax if both of the following conditions are met

The receipts that would otherwise be brought into account in calculating the club's property income for the period must not exceed £30,000. The threshold is proportionately reduced for accounting periods of less than 12 months. For accounting periods beginning before 1 April 2015 the threshold was £30,000. Periods which straddle 1 April 2015 are treated as two separate accounting periods and the receipts apportioned between them.

The second condition is that all of the UK property income for that period is applied for qualifying purposes (as above).

[CTA 2010, s 662; FA 2013, Sch 21 para 7; SI 2014 No 3327].

Interest, gift aid income and company gift income

A club that is a registered club throughout an accounting period can make a claim for its interest income, 'gift aid income' and, for payments made on or after 1 April 2014, 'company gift income' for the period to be exempt from corporation tax if the whole of the income is applied for qualifying purposes (as above). '*Gift aid income*' for this purpose means gifts to the club made by individuals which are qualifying gift aid donations. 'Company gift income' means gifts of money to the club made by companies which are not charities.

[CTA 2010, s 664; FA 2014, s 35(8)(10)(12)].

Chargeable gains

A gain accruing to a registered club is not a chargeable gain if it is wholly applied for qualifying purposes (as above) and the club makes a claim to that effect. [*CTA 2010, s 665*].

Where a club holds property and, without disposing of it, ceases at any time to be a registered club or to hold the property for qualifying purposes, it is treated for the purposes of *TCGA 1992* as having disposed of, and immediately reacquired, the property at that time at its then market value. Any gain resulting from the deemed disposal does not attract the above exemption. Additionally, to the extent that any of the property represents, directly or indirectly, the consideration for the disposal of assets by the club, any gain that accrued on that disposal does not attract the exemption. Assessments in respect of resulting chargeable gains can be made at any time not later than three years after the end of the accounting period in which falls the event giving rise to this treatment. [*CTA 2010, s 669*].

Restrictions on exemptions

The above exemptions are restricted where a registered club incurs any expenditure for non-qualifying purposes in an accounting period and any of the club's income or gains for that period are exempted from tax (or would be but for the restriction).

The restriction operates by comparing the amount of the expenditure incurred in the accounting period for non-qualifying purposes (*'the non-qualifying expenditure'*) with the aggregate of the club's income (whether or not taxable, and before deducting expenses) and gains (whether chargeable gains or gains exempted as above) for the accounting period (*'the total income and gains'*), as follows:

(1)   Where the non-qualifying expenditure is less than the total income and gains, the amount of exempt income and gains is restricted in the proportion that the non-qualifying expenditure bears to the total income and gains.

(2)   Where the non-qualifying expenditure equals the total income and gains, the amount of exempt income and gains is reduced to nil.

(3)   Where the non-qualifying expenditure exceeds the total income and gains, the amount of exempt income and gains is reduced to nil, and the 'surplus amount' is carried back to previous accounting periods (latest first) ending not more than six years before the end of the current period, and deducted from income and gains exempted for those periods. To the extent that the amount exempted for an accounting period has already been reduced under this provision or (1) or (2) above, it cannot be reduced again by reference to expenditure of a later accounting period. The *'surplus amount'* is the excess of:

(i)   an amount equal to the proportion of the originally exempt income and gains that the non-qualifying expenditure bears to the total income and gains, over;

(ii)   the amount of the originally exempt income and gains.

Where, as a consequence of this restriction, a registered club has an amount of income and gains for which exemption is not available, the club may, by notice to HMRC, specify which items of income and gains are, in whole or part, to be attributed to that amount. If no such notice is given by the club within 30 days of being required to do so by HMRC, it falls to HMRC to make the attribution.

[*CTA 2010, ss 666–668*].

Reliefs for donations

Gifts to registered clubs by individuals can qualify for relief under the gift aid provisions and gifts by companies can qualify for charitable donations relief (see **15.12** CHARITIES). Gifts received by a registered club which are qualifying gift aid donations are treated as received under deduction of income tax at the basic rate for the tax year in which the gift is made. See *CTA 2010, s 661D*.

Gifts of assets can qualify for relief under *TCGA 1992, s 257* (gifts of assets to charities treated as no gain/no loss).'

Investment clubs

[76.5] The text is amended to read as follows.

'An investment club comprises a group of people who have joined together to invest, primarily on the Stock Exchange. Members are entitled to a share of the income received on the investments and of the gains and losses on the disposal of any shares or other investments. Such clubs are generally unincorporated associations and therefore within the definition of a company for corporation tax purposes. However, HMRC consider that investment clubs generally hold funds in a fiduciary capacity and are therefore outside the scope of corporation tax (HMRC Company Taxation Manual CTM40650).

Each individual is charged to income tax and capital gains tax on his share of the income and gains. Income and gains can be measured either in accordance with rules agreed with HMRC for investment club purposes or under the usual rules. Under the former, the club adopts a standard agreement (available from HMRC) which allows each member to be charged to tax on a proportionate share of the club's income and gains. See HMRC Capital Gains Manual CG20600–CG20660.'

Key points on voluntary associations

[76.9] The key points are amended to read as follows.

'• A club may be established as a company or unincorporated society and be liable to corporation tax on income generated other than by members.
• Special rules apply to certain types of clubs.
• Registered community amateur sports clubs enjoy a number of tax advantages, including exemption from tax on UK trading profits and UK property income (up to certain limits) and on interest and gift aid income and chargeable gains. These tax exemptions are contingent on certain conditions being met.
• Clubs established by members for their own social and recreational purposes are not trading and as such are not liable to tax on any surplus of subscriptions over income. However any profit on commercial activities is taxable.
• Holiday clubs and thrift funds are outside the scope to tax.
• Members of investment clubs are taxed on income and gains arising from their investments. These may be computed according to normal rules or in accordance with a standard agreement with HMRC.
• Where a lottery is run to raise money for a sports club and a percentage of the ticket price is donated to the club, the donation element is excluded from the computation of profits for tax purposes.'

Spring Budget 2017

This is a summary of the most important tax changes in Spring Budget 2017. For more on the Budget, see the Spring Budget 2017 report and the Overview of tax legislation and rates 2017 ('OOTLAR') published by HM Treasury and HMRC (www.gov.uk/Government/publications/spring-budget-2017-overview -of-tax-legislation-and-rates-ootlar).

Personal and Business Tax

The highlights for individuals from the Spring Budget 2017 include:

- the making tax digital threshold for a one-year deferral in digital quarterly reporting will be the VAT threshold,
- the reduction in the dividend nil-rate band from £5,000 to £2,000 in 2018/19,
- the extension of the opportunity to clean-up mixed funds held by non-domiciliaries to cover pre-6 April 2008 foreign income and capital,
- a 25% tax charge on pension transfers to a qualifying recognised overseas pension scheme (QROPS) which take place on or after 9 March 2017.

Personal tax rates and allowances – 2017/18 tax year

Income tax allowances

Personal allowance	£11,500
Income limit for personal allowance	£100,000
Transferable tax allowance (also known as marriage allowance)	£1,150
Married couple's allowance (born before 6 April 1935)	£8,445
Minimum amount of married couple's allowance	£3,260
Income limit for married couple's allowance	£28,000
Blind person's allowance	£2,320

Income tax rates and taxable bands

Rate	
Starting rate for savings: 0%	£1–£5,000
Basic rate: 20%	£1–£33,500
Higher rate: 40%	£33,501–£150,000
Additional rate: 45%	Over £150,000

The savings rates are 0% (starting rate for savings), 0% (savings nil-rate band of £1,000 for basic rate taxpayers and £500 for higher rate taxpayers), 20% (savings basic rate), 40% (savings higher rate), 45% (savings additional rate).

The dividend rates are 0% (dividend nil rate on first £5,000 of dividend income), 7.5% (dividend ordinary rate), 32.5% (dividend upper rate) and 38.1% (dividend additional rate).

In 2017/18 the higher rate will kick in at an income level (before personal allowances) of £45,000 (rather than £43,000 as in 2016/17). This is the biggest above inflation increase to the threshold since it was introduced in 1989.

Scottish taxpayers – income tax bands

The Scottish Government has the power to vary the basic rate, higher rate and additional rate of income tax for non-savings income. It can also create new tax bands. It does not have the power to set the level of the personal allowance, set different rates for different types of income or alter/create/abolish income tax reliefs. These remain reserved by the UK Government.

As was widely expected, the Scottish higher rate threshold (personal allowance plus Scottish basic rate band) in 2017/18 is to be lower than the threshold which applies in the rest of the UK. The Scottish higher rate threshold will be £43,000 in 2017/18 (frozen at the 2016/17 level). The rates of tax and other thresholds remain the same as in the rest of the UK.

This creates a number of mismatches for Scottish taxpayers:

Mismatch	Commentary
Class 1 and Class 4 national insurance contributions	The upper earnings limit for Class 1 and the upper profits limit for Class 4 are aligned with the higher rate threshold which applies in the rest of the UK. Therefore, employed Scottish taxpayers will face a marginal rate of 52% on earnings between £43,000 and £45,000 (Scottish higher rate of 40% plus Class 1 primary rate of 12%). The marginal rate for the self-employed at this profit level will be 49% (Scottish higher rate of 40% plus Class 4 main rate of 9%).
Savings income and dividend income	The income tax rates and thresholds for the savings and dividend income of Scottish taxpayers are the same as for taxpayers in the rest of the UK. This means the starting rate for savings, savings nil-rate band and dividend nil-rate band should be considered for Scottish taxpayers. It also means that Scottish taxpayers may be higher rate taxpayers for non-savings income but basic rate taxpayers for savings income.

Mismatch	Commentary
Rates of capital gains tax	The rate of capital gains tax depends on the remaining basic rate band for income tax. The higher rate threshold for capital gains tax for Scottish taxpayers will remain aligned with the higher rate threshold for the rest of the UK. Therefore it is possible to be a higher rate taxpayer in Scotland but have remaining basic rate band for the purposes of capital gains tax.

National insurance rates and thresholds

Lower earnings limit, primary Class 1	£113
Upper earnings limit, primary Class 1	£866
Primary threshold	£157
Secondary threshold	£157
Upper secondary threshold	£866
Employment allowance (per employer)	£3,000 per year
Employees' primary Class 1 rate between primary threshold and upper earnings limit	12%
Employees' primary Class 1 rate above upper earnings limit	2%
Employers' secondary Class 1 rate above secondary threshold	13.8%
Class 1A rate on employer-provided benefits	13.8%
Class 1B rate on amounts included in a PAYE settlement agreement	13.8%
Class 2 rate	£2.85
Class 2 small profits threshold	£6,025 per year
Class 3 rate	£14.25
Class 4 lower profits limit	£8,164 per year
Class 4 upper profits limit	£45,000 per year
Class 4 rate between lower profits limit and upper profits limit	9%
Class 4 rate above upper profits limit	2%

There is an exemption from secondary Class 1 national insurance contributions (NIC) in relation to employees under 21 and apprentices under 25 years old. The exemption applies until the employee's earnings reach the upper secondary threshold, at which point secondary contributions are due.

Note that the ability to make voluntary Class 3A contributions ceases on 5 April 2017. This was a temporary class of NIC introduced to give people who reached state pension age before 6 April 2016 the opportunity to build up their state pension entitlement by up to £25 per week.

Capital gains tax rates and exempt amount

The annual exempt amount for capital gains tax is increased to £11,300 in 2017/18. The annual exempt amount for trustees in 2017/18 is £5,650.

The capital gains tax rates remain the same for individuals, personal representatives and trustees as they were in 2016/17. The main rates are 10% for basic rate taxpayers and 20% for higher rate taxpayers, trustees and personal representatives. The 'upper rates' of 18% (basic rate taxpayers) and 28% (higher rate taxpayers, trustees and personal representatives) apply to gains on residential property and carried interest. The rate of tax for ATED-related gains remains 28%.

Inheritance tax

The nil-rate band remains £325,000 and the rate of inheritance tax remains unchanged. As announced in Summer Budget 2015, the nil-rate band will remain frozen until 2021/22 at the earliest.

The residence nil-rate band is phased in from 2017/18. The residence nil-rate band applies to reduce the inheritance tax payable on death but is restricted to the value of residential property included in the death estate which is passed to direct descendants.

The amount of the residence nil-rate band available where the date of death falls in 2017/18 is £100,000.

Business owners

Dividend nil rate

Introduced from 2016/17, the dividend nil-rate band (also referred to as the dividend allowance) taxes the first £5,000 of dividend income at 0%, irrespective of the taxpayer's marginal tax rate. At the time it was speculated that this both acted as a simplification measure for the making tax digital agenda and a sweetener for the increase in the effective tax rates for dividend income introduced at the same time.

Given the level of the dividend nil-rate band it is not surprising that the taxpayers who benefitted most from this measure were owner-managers of companies.

As part of the aim to reduce the tax incentive for incorporation, from 2018/19 the dividend nil-rate band will be reduced to £2,000. The Chancellor asserts that at this level most general investors will still pay no tax on their dividends.

It is therefore essential to ensure that individuals maximise their use of the £5,000 dividend nil-rate band in 2017/18.

Appropriations into trading stock

If a trader transfers a business asset into trading stock, the cost of the stock for the purpose of the accounts is the market value at the time it was appropriated. For capital gains purposes, the trader is deemed to have sold the fixed asset at market value. In this instance the trader can elect not to have a capital gains tax disposal but instead to have the cost of the stock reduced by the amount of the chargeable gain. This will reduce the gain to nil but will result in the stock having a lower cost (and therefore a higher trading profit when the stock is eventually sold).

For transfers on or after 8 March 2017, it is no longer possible to make such an election where an allowable loss would arise on an appropriation into trading stock at market value. This means that an allowable loss will be crystallised when the appropriation takes place, and the loss will remain within the capital gains tax rules with respect to how it may be set off in the future. The aim of this provision is to remove the ability of business with loss-making capital assets to obtain an unfair tax advantage by converting those losses into more flexible trading losses.

Where traders have more than one asset they wish to appropriate as trading stock, it will be sensible to consider the timing of this. Where one asset stands at a gain, and one at a loss, it may be advantageous to appropriate the asset standing at a gain before or at the same time as the asset standing at a loss and make no election. This will ensure that the loss arising can be utilised more effectively within the capital gains tax rules.

Partnership tax treatment

Following the August 2016 consultation, Finance Bill 2018 will contain provisions which clarify some aspects of partnership taxation, particularly in relation to profit allocations. The Government is aware that some of the existing rules are unclear or produce an inappropriate outcome and wishes to make both the calculation and reporting of profits simpler. A summary of responses is also expected.

Simplified cash basis for small unincorporated businesses

In line with the summary of responses, with effect from 6 April 2017 the entry and exit thresholds for the simplified cash basis for small unincorporated businesses are being increased. The entry threshold will increase from £83,000 to £150,000. The exit threshold will be £300,000. For Universal Credit claimants both the entry and exit thresholds will be £300,000.

At the same time the rules for deductible capital expenditure under the simplified cash basis will be clarified via the introduction of a statutory list of disallowed expenditure. For 2017/18 profits can be calculated using either the new rules or the existing rules.

Following consultation on the draft legislation, the Finance Bill 2017 clauses will be revised to ensure the rules on the movement from the cash basis to the accruals basis are 'robust'.

Employee issues

Valuation of benefits in kind

As expected from Autumn Statement 2016, the Government will:

* launch a consultation on the valuation of living accommodation,
* publish a call for evidence on the valuation of all other benefits in kind.

Relief for business expenses

A call for evidence will be published in the Finance Bill on the use of income tax relief for employees' business expenses, including those not reimbursed by the employer.

Termination payments

The following changes are to be made to the income tax and NIC treatment of termination payments from 6 April 2018:

- removal of the distinction between the taxation of contractual and non-contractual payments in lieu of notice (PILONs) and make all PILONs both taxable and subject to Class 1 NIC (primary and secondary contributions),
- retention of the £30,000 threshold for termination payments but amounts above that would be subject to secondary Class 1 NIC (no primary Class 1 contributions will be payable by the employee) as well as income tax,
- removal of foreign service relief (except in the case of seafarers).

Although these measures were pre-announced, it is now understood that whilst the bulk of the changes will be legislated in Finance Bill 2017 and NIC Bill 2017 as planned, the abolition of foreign service relief will be deferred to Finance Bill 2018 based on responses to the draft legislation.

Enterprise management incentives

The Government is to seek state aid approval to extend the tax reliefs associated with the enterprise management incentive (EMI) scheme beyond 2018. The last time state aid approval was granted to this scheme was in August 2009.

Property owners

Simplified cash basis for unincorporated businesses

As stated in the January 2017 summary of responses, the simplified cash basis will be extended to unincorporated property businesses from 6 April 2017.

This will be the default method of calculating the property income, unless:

- the landlord makes an election not to use the simplified cash basis (separate elections must be made for different types of property businesses),
- the gross rental income exceeds £150,000,
- the business is carried on by a company, an LLP, a partnership with a corporate partner, a trust or personal representatives,
- business premises renovation allowances have been claimed and there is a balancing adjustment in the tax year.

For those property businesses unwilling or unable to use the simplified cash basis, the accruals basis must be used to calculate the property income.

Where property is owned jointly by spouses or civil partners, if one spouse or civil partner makes an election for the accruals basis to apply then the other spouse/civil partner is excluded from using the simplified cash basis. For all other jointly owned property, each owner can choose whether to elect to use the accruals basis or to remain on the simplified cash basis.

The simplified cash basis for unincorporated property businesses is closely modelled on the simplified cash basis for unincorporated trading businesses, however there are some important differences:

- interest is allowed as a deduction without the application of the £500 limit and the related mixed purpose interest rule (instead interest will be allowed according to the existing rules for landlords, including the restriction of relief for interest in relation to residential properties starting in 2017/18),
- the continued ability to deduct the cost of replacing domestic items in residential properties which applies from 2016/17. The initial cost of capital items used in a dwelling house will not be an allowable expense under the simplified cash basis in the same way as this is not permitted under the accruals basis.

Landlords should consider carefully whether the cash basis is beneficial to them. Whilst simplified accounting may be tempting it could create other issues, particularly in relation to the timing of receipts. For example, if a tenant pays a full year's rent in advance on 31 March then the entire amount must be included in the profits for that year, which could impact areas such as the high income child benefit charge or the abatement of the personal allowance where the adjusted net income exceeds £100,000.

Rent-a-room relief

In a surprise announcement, in summer 2017 the Government will launch a consultation on rent-a-room relief, with a view to better supporting longer-term lodgings.

The reference to longer-term lodging may suggest that the conditions for rent-a-room relief could be altered to ensure it applies to long-term lets only. Currently anyone letting a room in their home on a short-term basis using sharing websites such as Airbnb can receive up to £7,500 per year in rents without paying income tax. When rent-a-room relief was introduced in 1992, this type of short-term letting could not be envisaged and the Government may decide this does not meet the original policy objective.

Non-domiciliaries

At Summer Budget 2015 Chancellor Osborne announced fundamental changes to the tax regime for non-domiciled individuals. They involve deeming an individual to be UK domiciled for tax purposes even though he may be non-domiciled in the UK under general law. The rules will apply for income tax, capital gains tax (CGT) and inheritance tax (IHT).

From 2017/18 it is expected that an individual will be deemed UK domiciled for income tax and CGT:

- if he has been UK resident for at least 15 out of the last 20 tax years, or
- if he was born in the UK with a UK domicile of origin, subsequently left the UK and acquired a non-UK domicile of choice and later becomes resident in the UK

The 20-year 'look-back' period for 2017/18 is 1997/98 to 2016/17. The 'clock' does not restart from 2017/18.

Following the responses to the initial consultation, it was announced that non-domiciliaries:

- caught by the deemed domicile 15-year rule in 2017/18 will be able to rebase their foreign chargeable assets for CGT purposes as at 5 April 2017,
- will have a one-off opportunity to clean-up existing mixed funds within foreign bank accounts (transfers out should be made between 6 April 2017 and 5 April 2019).

Whilst both these measures are good news for the non-domiciliary, they have underlying traps for the unwary that were not obvious at the time of the original announcements.

Clean-up of mixed funds

The change announced affects the cleansing of mixed funds. Based on the latest draft legislation, released on 26 January 2017, it was pointed out by the Chartered Institute of Taxation that mixed funds containing pre-6 April 2008 income and/or capital were excluded from the clean-up. CIOT response (23 Feb 2017), paras 14.6–14.9.

It is confirmed that the Finance Bill 2017 clauses will be amended to include such mixed funds within the opportunity. This probably reflects the original policy intention, since excluding such mixed funds would severely limit its usefulness.

However several uncertainties remain, including: (i) whether it will be possible to clean-up mixed funds based on reasonable estimates of foreign income and capital rather than absolute certainty and (ii) how to determine the composition of any funds remaining in the original bank account following the transfers out. Whilst it is possible that this may be ironed out in the Finance Bill 2017 clauses due for publication on 20 March 2017, it is likely that others will be covered in the subsequent HMRC guidance. Some advisers may, therefore, decide to wait for the publication of the HMRC guidance before beginning to split out mixed funds. The fact that the time limit has been extended to 5 April 2019 (from the originally proposed deadline of 5 April 2018) is helpful here.

Pensions

Money purchase annual allowance

As announced in Autumn Statement 2016, the money purchase annual allowance (MPAA) will be reduced from £10,000 to £4,000. The MPAA is only triggered when a pension scheme member draws income from a flexi-access drawdown fund and it exists to prevent the member reinvesting this money back into a pension, thus obtaining double income tax relief.

Note that the MPAA is **not** triggered if:

- the member uses the tax-free lump sum only and does not draw income from the taxable portion of the fund,
- the member's fund is still held under the former 'capped drawdown' arrangement and the withdrawals of income do not exceed the capped amount (if the cap is exceeded, the drawdown fund automatically converts to flexi-access in any case).

Provided members can keep their withdrawals within these conditions, the standard annual allowance of £40,000 applies.

The summary of responses to the November 2016 consultation was expected to be published on 20 March 2017.

Foreign pensions

The announcement at Autumn Statement 2016 that the tax treatment of foreign pensions would be 'more closely aligned' with the UK's domestic pension tax regime was broadly interpreted as being notice that the rule under which only 90% of foreign pension income is subject to UK income tax would be abolished. This was confirmed as correct by the draft legislation published in December 2016.

Specialist schemes for those employed abroad (known as 'section 615' schemes) will be closed to new saving but any lump sums paid out in relation to funds built up before 6 April 2017 will be subject to the current tax treatment.

Foreign pensions – QROPS

A 25% tax charge will be levied on pension transfers to a qualifying recognised overseas pension scheme (QROPS) which take place on or after 9 March 2017.

Although the legitimate use of QROPS is acknowledged, it is noted that the transfer of funds which have benefited from UK income tax relief has provided an opportunity for a tax advantage. QROPS can be located in a lower tax jurisdiction or one which offers less restrictive withdrawal rules. As a result, QROPS schemes have been marketed as tax saving vehicles. The new law aims to preserve the legitimate purpose of transferring pension schemes, whilst penalising the tax avoidance motive.

'Genuine' transfers will be identified if they meet one of the following conditions:

- the QROPS and the person who makes the transfer are resident in the same country, or
- the QROPS and the person who makes the transfer are both resident in a country within the European Economic Area, or
- the transfer is made to a QROPS that is established or sponsored by the employer of the person who makes the transfer.

Transfers which do not meet these conditions will incur a charge of 25% of the value of the transferred.

There will be a five-year window following the transfer during which:

- a transfer which was not chargeable will become so if it ceases to meet the qualifying conditions regarding residence, and
- a charge which was made can be refunded if one of the qualifying conditions starts to apply,
- payments out of the QROPS will be subject to UK tax rules regardless of where the individual then resides.

The administrators of both the UK scheme and the QROPS will be jointly and severally liable to the tax charge. It is expected that it will be deducted from the pension fund on transfer.

Tax planning with QROPS is a niche area, popular with wealthy and internationally mobile individuals. Advisers with clients who may be affected by these changes are advised to study the draft legislation and HMRC guidance at an early stage in view of the immediate changes in the law. Existing QROPS have an early deadline of 13 April 2017 to decide whether they wish to maintain their status.

Investments

ISAs

The ISA limit will be £20,000 in 2017/18 (up from £15,420 in 2016/17), as previously trailed in Budget 2016. The Chancellor used this above inflation increase to partly justify his reduction to the dividend nil-rate band; individuals can purchase shares via an ISA to benefit from the tax-free wrapper.

Venture capital schemes

As announced in Autumn Statement 2016, further minor tweaks to the rules for enterprise investment schemes (EIS), venture capital trusts (VCTs) and seed enterprise investment schemes (SEIS) are expected in Finance Bill 2017:

- clarification to the rules for share conversion rights (for EIS and SEIS shares issued on or after 5 December 2016), which means that the 'no pre-arranged exits' requirement will not apply if a right exists for the conversion or exchange of shares at some future date,
- aligning the VCT rules for follow-on funding to match the rules for EIS,
- a power to enable the rules on share-for-share exchanges for VCTs to be made via secondary legislation.

The summary of responses to the December 2015 consultation on ways of improving the advance assurance service for venture capital schemes is expected to follow the Spring Budget 2017.

Social investments tax relief

As partially announced in Autumn Statement 2016 and further to the draft legislation published on 26 January 2017, the following changes to social investments tax relief (SITR) will apply to investments made on or after 6 April 2017:

- the investment limit for qualifying social enterprises aged up to seven years old will increase to £1.5m,
- the list of excluded activities will be tightened up to include asset leasing and on-lending. Whilst nursing homes and residential care homes will also be classed as excluded activities, the Government intends to revisit these activities in future with the aim of introducing an accreditation system which will allow fundraising via SITR,
- the limit on the number of full-time equivalent employees will be reduced from 500 to 250,
- the use of money raised under the SITR to pay off existing loans will be excluded,
- the law will be clarified so that individuals will be eligible to claim relief under the SITR only if they are independent from the social enterprise,
- a provision will be introduced to exclude investments where arrangements are put in place with the main purpose of delivering a benefit to an individual or party connected to the social enterprise.

Life insurance policies

As expected, legislation will be introduced in Finance Bill 2017 to change the taxation of partial surrenders from life insurance policies in order to prevent excessive tax charges. However, it is interesting that despite consulting on three options, in the end the draft legislation published in December 2016 contained a remedy which was not mentioned in the consultation. Any policy holder who has inadvertently triggered a disproportionate gain will be able to apply to HMRC to have the chargeable event gain recalculated on a just and reasonable basis.

However, the fact that the draft legislation was built around an option which had not been subject to consultation meant that uncertainties remained over the operation of the provision. As such, following comments received, the Finance Bill 2017 clauses will be revised to clarify who can apply, when the application can be made and how the recalculation is to be given effect. These rules will apply from Royal Assent to Finance Act 2017.

Whether this will address the other concerns raised, such as the lack of a statutory right of appeal, remains to be seen.

Savings bonds

As expected, National Savings and Investments (NS&I) will launch a new three-year savings bond in April 2017. It was confirmed in the Spring Budget 2017 that the interest rate will be 2.2% per annum. The bond will be open to those over 16 years of age and the maximum investment will be £3,000. This interest rate is significantly higher than the rates offered by banks and building societies for mainstream savings products and there is likely to be a high take-up amongst basic rate and higher rate taxpayers (who also benefit from the savings nil-rate band).

Administration

Making tax digital

Under making tax digital, businesses will be required to file quarterly income and expense reports digitally. For many businesses this will represent significant extra administration work plus the cost of buying an appropriate software package and extra accountancy fees.

Based on the threshold for the one-year deferral announced in Spring Budget 2017, the main timescales for mandation will be:

* April 2018 – unincorporated businesses (including unincorporated property businesses) with a turnover above the VAT registration threshold (for their income tax obligations only),
* April 2019 – unincorporated businesses (including unincorporated property businesses) with a turnover above £10,000 but below the VAT registration threshold (for their income tax obligations) **plus** all businesses (unincorporated and incorporated) for their VAT obligations,
* April 2020 – all incorporated businesses for their corporation tax obligations.

The use of the VAT threshold as the level for the one-year deferral of quarterly digital reporting is a significant and very welcome development. Anecdotal evidence suggested that HMRC had been reluctant to entertain the idea of using the VAT threshold during the consultation process and it is to its credit that it has listened to advisers on this matter.

For unincorporated businesses it is expected that these requirements will apply to the accounting period beginning on or after 6 April of the relevant year. Therefore, for unincorporated trading businesses it may be possible to extend the deferral period by changing their accounting date. For example a business with turnover below the VAT threshold and an accounting date of 31 March will not have to make quarterly digital reports until the accounting period beginning 1 April 2020. Consideration should of course be given to the change of accounting date rules.

It is not possible to change the accounting date for an unincorporated property business as the income must be reported on a tax year basis.

Making tax digital – tax administration

A further consultation on late submission penalties under the making tax digital regime was due to be published on 20 March 2017.

At the same time, the Government will also consult on the 'design aspects of the tax administration system', with the aim of a consistent approach across the taxes. However it would appear from the draft legislation on administration published in January 2017 that we can expect amendments to be made to the existing statutes rather than using making tax digital as an opportunity for a total rethink of tax administration from a 21st Century perspective.

NIC – collection of arrears

It was announced at Autumn Statement 2016 that from April 2018 NIC would no longer be covered by the Limitation Act 1980. However, this is now expected to be delayed to allow for full consultation. Currently if HMRC wants to recover NIC debt it must raise a protective assessment within six years of the end of the tax year in question. The collection of arrears of tax is not covered by the Limitation Act 1980 so this leads to a mismatch in dealing with historic tax investigations where there is an associated NIC liability.

This is an interesting measure as it will enable HMRC to collect more NIC arrears, but by aligning the treatment for tax and NIC it means it can be badged as a simplification measure and a step towards income tax and NIC alignment.

Note that the position in Scotland is different. There it is already possible to collect NIC debt going back 20 years.

Income tax allowances for property and trading income

The £1,000 'allowances' for property and trading income, previously announced in Budget 2016, come into force in 2017/18. The trading income allowance also covers miscellaneous income from the provision of assets or services.

These work in a similar way to rent-a-room relief in that the first £1,000 of gross trading or property income will be exempt from income tax. If the income exceeds £1,000 the taxpayer will have a choice of:

- deducting the £1,000 'allowance' from their gross income and being taxable on the excess, or
- deducting allowable expenses in the normal way.

To utilise the allowance, the individual must make an election by the first anniversary of 31 January after the end of the tax year (e.g. 31 January 2020 for the 2017/18 tax year).

However, following consultation on the draft legislation published in December 2016, changes will be made in Finance Bill 2017 to prevent the allowances from applying to:

- the income of a participator in a connected close company,
- partnership income.

Employment Taxes

Both generally and from the perspective of employers and their advisers, the spring Budget was refreshingly light on tax measures. Details of those which were included can be found in Chapter 3 of the Spring Budget 2017 document and supported by the OOTLAR which summarises all changes in the pipeline, including those previously announced.

Company cars

There were no changes announced to the company car tax rates that will apply from 2017/18 to 2020/21 as already either enacted or announced in the Autumn Statement.

National Living Wage/National Minimum Wage

The Chancellor in the Budget announced that the National Living Wage will be increased to £7.50 per hour from April 2017. The following table shows all minimum wage rates for all age groups:

Category	Current rate	New rate from 1 April 2017
Workers 25 and over	£7.20 per hour	£7.50 per hour
21–24 year olds	£6.95 per hour	£7.05 per hour
18–20 year olds	£5.55 per hour	£5.60 per hour
16–17 year olds	£4.00 per hour	£4.05 per hour
Apprentices	£3.40 per hour	£3.50 per hour
Accommodation offset	£6.00 per day	£6.40 per day

Personal service companies ('IR35')

As announced in last year's Budget, as from 6 April 2017, where a worker provides his services through a personal service company (PSC) to a public sector body, it will be up to the public sector body (or the agency responsible for paying the PSC) to decide whether or not the special rules for PSCs (known as the IR35 rules) should apply. If the IR35 rules do apply, then the public sector body or agency will deduct the tax due on the resulting deemed employment income payment from the amount due to the PSC under the contract.

In a recent change to proposals for how the public sector body (or agency) should calculate the deemed employment payment, it will be up to them whether they take account of the worker's expenses in calculating that amount. If the expenses are left out of account the worker could still claim a deduction for qualifying expenses in the normal way.

The outline of this measure is covered in HMRC's tax information and impact note.

The list of public bodies who will assume this new responsibility as from 6 April was included as Annex B to the consultation document on this change in approach.

HMRC has also recently published a revised Employment Status Tool to help anyone considering the position of a worker providing services through a PSC to decide whether or not the IR35 rules apply.

Dividend nil-rate band reduction

In a step ostensibly aimed at addressing the unfairness in the differences in tax treatment between employees and those who provide their services through a limited company, the Chancellor announced that the dividend nil-rate band will reduce from £5,000 to £2,000 from 6 April 2018. Although this will indeed impact on the users of personal service companies, it will have a wider impact, affecting anyone receiving dividends of over £2,000 a year, including shareholder directors/employees of many smaller companies.

Pensions

The Budget did not include any new proposals in respect of the lifetime allowance or annual allowance for pension contributions.

However, employers of internationally mobile employees may well want to be aware that there is a new 25% charge on pension scheme members if they make a transfer from a UK-registered pension scheme to a Qualifying Recognised Overseas Pension Scheme (QROPS). It will apply to transfers taking place on or after 9 March 2017. This charge does not apply if **any** of the following apply:

• the member is resident in the same country in which the QROPS receiving the transfer is established,
• the member is resident in a country within the European Economic Area (EEA) and the QROPS is established in a country within the EEA,
• the QROPS is an occupational pension scheme sponsored by the individual's employer,
• the QROPS is an overseas public service pension scheme and the member is an employee of an employer that participates in the scheme,
• the QROPS is set up by an international organisation to provide benefits for or in respect of past service as an employee of the organisation and the member is an employee of that international organisation.

This means that an employee making a transfer from a registered scheme into a QROPS as a consequence of a cross-border change in employment will often be outside the new charge.

Other changes to be included in Finance Bill 2017

The OOTLAR document includes confirmation that a number of previously announced measures of particular interest to employers are still on course to be included in Finance Bill 2017.

Benefits in kind

During the summer last year there was a consultation on proposals to align the date for 'making good' on benefits in kind. If an employee 'makes good' (repays) an amount to the employer in respect of a benefit in kind, the cash equivalent is reduced by the amount made good. The date by which the employee must 'make good' in order to reduce a benefit varies according to the benefit provided.

In para 1.6 of OOTLAR, HMRC confirms that Finance Bill 2017 will include legislation to set the aligned date to be 6 July following the end of the tax year. This change will apply for benefits provided in 2017/18 onwards.

Salary sacrifice

With effect from 6 April 2017, salary sacrifice arrangements, described as 'optional remuneration arrangements', may be used to achieve tax and NIC savings only in the case of:

- employer pension contributions and advice,
- employer-provided childcare,
- cycle-to-work schemes,
- ultra-low emission company cars.

Transitional provisions apply where the salary sacrifice arrangement was in place before 6 April 2017. See para 1.7 of OOTLAR.

Termination payments

The Autumn Statement last year included details of the expected changes to the treatment of termination payments. In para 1.8 of today's OOTLAR, HMRC indicates that although the main changes to the tax and NIC treatment of termination payments will be legislated in the Finance Bill 2017, proposals to abolish foreign service relief will be deferred to the Finance Bill 2018.

Proposal dropped – sanction for hiring illegal workers

In last year's Budget the Chancellor announced an intention to temporarily deny the NIC employment allowance to employers taking on workers who do not have a legal right to work in the UK. Following consultation, this proposal has been dropped. Any employer taking on such workers already faces significant civil penalties of up to £20,000 per illegal worker.

Upcoming consultations

The OOTLAR document gives details of a number of consultations on possible future changes to employment taxes, due to be published on 20 March 2017:

- a call for evidence on employees' expenses,
- consultation on proposal to modernise the tax treatment of employer-provided living accommodation and board and lodgings

a call for evidence on exemptions and valuation methodology for employer-provided benefits in kind.

Corporation Tax

In the spirit of moving towards a single fiscal event in the autumn, the Spring Budget 2017 does not set out major changes to the taxation of companies. Minor amendments have been made to a number of announcements made in previous years, details of which are provided below.

Further information on some of the announcements will be available when the Finance Bill 2017 is published.

Appropriations to trading stock

Currently, if a fixed asset is appropriated into trading stock, then the 'cost' of the stock for the purposes of the accounts is the market value at the time it was introduced. For chargeable gains purposes, there is a deemed disposal of the fixed asset at market value. In this instance an election can be made to reduce the cost of the stock by the amount of the chargeable gain, rather than triggering a disposal. This will reduce the gain to nil but will result in the stock having a lower cost, and therefore a higher trading profit, when the stock is eventually sold.

For transfers made on or after 8 March 2017, it is no longer possible to make such an election where an allowable loss would arise on an appropriation into trading stock at market value. This means that an allowable loss will be crystallised when the appropriation takes place, and the loss will remain within the chargeable gains rules with respect to how it may be set off in the future. The aim of this provision is to remove the ability of businesses with loss making capital assets to obtain an unfair tax advantage by converting those losses into more flexible trading losses.

Where companies have more than one asset that may be appropriated to trading stock, it will be sensible to consider the timing of any appropriation. Where one asset stands at a gain, and one at a loss, it may be advantageous to appropriate the asset standing at a gain before or at the same time as the asset standing at a loss and make no election. This will ensure that the loss arising can be utilised more effectively within the chargeable gains rules.

Review of R&D regime

The UK has a comprehensive regime to encourage companies to invest in research and development.

Following a review, the Government has announced that administrative changes will be made to the research and development expenditure credit (RDEC) to increase certainty and to simplify claims. Action will also be taken to increase awareness of R&D tax credits among SMEs. Further details on the changes, or indeed when they are likely to have effect, have not been provided.

Offshore property developers

Legislation was introduced by Finance Act 2016, ss 76–77 to ensure non-resident developers of UK land are subject to UK corporation tax on the profits generated by this activity. This was intended to create a level playing field between UK and foreign-based developers. The original legislation excluded profits arising from contracts entered into before 5 July 2016. The Government did not anticipate that profits arising many months or years later as a result of these contracts would not be subject to UK corporation tax. Amendments have been made to ensure that all profits recognised in a period of account beginning on or after 8 March 2017 are taxed irrespective of when the contract was entered into. Where the period of account straddles 8 March 2017, then the amounts arising between 8 March 2017 and the end of the straddling period are also taxed.

Plant and machinery leasing

Current rules under GAAP treat leased assets as either finance leases or operating leases. Finance leases are capitalised on the balance sheet as fixed assets, with a matching lease obligation in creditors. Assets subject to operating leases are off balance sheet assets.

IFRS 16, which is the new leasing standard issued by the International Accounting Standards Board, comes into effect on 1 January 2019. This standard will radically alter the GAAP treatment of lessees of most assets, although lessors will still maintain a distinction between finance and operating leases. There are exceptions within the standard for leases of 12 months or less and low value items.

The impact for lessees will be to increase the level of debt and the value of the asset base on the balance sheet, as all leases must be capitalised. The timing of debits recognised in the accounts on operating leases will be accelerated, even though the payments for hire of the asset are likely to be uniform over the lease. Rental expenses on leases which are currently classified as operating leases will be replaced by depreciation and front loaded interest charges. Companies using IFRS may need to model the effect on their gearing, earnings per share and debt covenants as well as many other financial metrics and ratios.

The Government will launch a consultation in Summer 2017, building on the discussion document published in Summer 2016. The Government intends to maintain the current system of lease taxation, rather than changing the tax system to match the accounting. This would seem to be the most sensible approach as it should avoid awkward and complex transitional adjustments. However, one downside of this approach will be to create differences between the P&L debits and the amounts deductible for tax, requiring greater measurement and tracking of temporary differences within deferred tax.

It should be noted that some changes to the rules on long funding leases and certain anti-avoidance rules on leasing will be required as they are linked to current accounting definitions.

Withholding tax amendments

Withholding tax exemption for debt traded on multilateral trading facility

UK tax at the basic rate of 20% must be withheld from certain payments of annual interest. It was announced that an exemption will be introduced for interest on debt traded on a multilateral trading facility. The purpose of the exemption, which is subject to consultation in Spring 2017, is to further the development of UK debt markets.

Double taxation treaty passport scheme

HMRC launched a Double Taxation Treaty Passport (DTTP) scheme for overseas corporate lenders applicable to loans taken out on or after 1 September 2010. The lender must be resident in a country with which the UK has a double taxation treaty that includes an interest or income from a debt claim article. The existence of a 'Treaty Passport' simplifies the process whereby a UK borrower is able to access reduced rates of withholding tax. In order to assist businesses with raising finance, the Government announced today an intention to renew and extend the administrative simplifications of the DTTP scheme. Guidance and the revised terms and conditions applying to the scheme will be published on GOV.UK on 6 April 2017.

Large business risk review

A consultation document is due to be published in Summer 2017 which aims to review HMRC's processes for assessing the risk profile of large businesses. The Government also wants to consider ways of promoting stronger compliance. Unfortunately, further details have not been provided alongside today's announcement.

Patient capital

'Patient capital' is a term used to describe a long-term capital investment in a growing innovative business. The investor is willing to make a financial investment in a business with no expectation of generating a quick profit, however it is possible that more substantial returns will be generated at some point in the future.

The Patient Capital Review was launched by HM Treasury and the Department for Business, Energy & Industrial Strategy (BEIS) in January 2017 as part of the Government's aim to build a modern industrial strategy. The review did not previously include consideration of the tax measures linked with patient capital for growing businesses. The Chancellor announced today that a consultation will be launched in Spring 2017, which will review the tax reliefs aimed at encouraging investment and entrepreneurship. Specific reliefs have not been mentioned, but it is assumed that it could include EIS reliefs, SEIS reliefs, VCT reliefs, entrepreneurs' relief and investors' relief.

The final recommendations from the review will be presented to the Chancellor ahead of Autumn Budget 2017.

Creative sector tax reliefs

It was confirmed today that the Government will seek State Aid approval for the continued provision of high-end television, animation and video games tax reliefs beyond 2018.

Amendments to measures previously announced

A number of measures that have been announced in the past are subject to minor amendments. Details are provided below.

Deductibility of interest

Following announcements at Budget 2016, plus a period of consultation, draft legislation was published on 5 December 2016 and 26 January 2017 to restrict the tax deduction available to companies in respect of interest and similar items.

From 1 April 2017, a group will have its interest expense restricted to a maximum deduction of 30% of earnings before interest, tax, depreciation and amortisation (EBITDA) that is taxable in the UK. The legislation also includes a modified debt cap replacing the existing worldwide debt cap to ensure that the UK net interest deduction cannot exceed the total net interest expense of the worldwide group. An optional group ratio rule based on the net interest to EBITDA ratio of the worldwide group may result in a greater deduction in some circumstances.

Alternative rules apply to infrastructure companies which may have the effect of largely taking them outside the rules with no interest restriction even though they may be highly geared.

Groups with net interest expense of £2m or less will be unaffected by these rules.

The Government has announced a series of detailed amendments to eliminate 'unintended consequences' and reduce 'unnecessary compliance burdens' as follows:

- changes to the modified debt cap to prevent certain restrictions for carried forward interest expenses,
- the alternative rules for public infrastructure groups will be simplified to eliminate the need to compare levels of indebtedness of non-qualifying group companies. Transitional rules will apply in the first year to allow any necessary restructuring to obtain the more favourable alternative treatment,
- the rules on guaranteed debt have been amended including those in relation to intra-group guarantees,
- income and expenses from dealing in financial instruments will be included in the definition of interest for banking trades,
- special rules will allow insurers to compute interest on an amortised cost basis as an alternative to fair value accounting.

These changes will be reflected in Finance Bill 2017 and will have effect from 1 April 2017.

Reform of the substantial shareholdings exemption (SSE)

Following a period of consultation, amendments will be made to the SSE reforms included in the draft Finance Bill 2017, which were originally announced at Autumn Statement 2016. Whilst we do not yet have details, the latest changes are expected to provide further clarity and certainty and take effect from 1 April 2017.

Reform of loss relief

Reforms to the loss relief regime were originally announced at Budget 2016. Legislation was included in the draft Finance Bill 2017, with further draft legislation published on 26 January 2017. The latest changes include provisions for oil and gas companies and oil contractors. All reforms take effect from 1 April 2017.

Patent box

It was announced at Autumn Statement 2016 that the patent box rules would be revised by Finance Bill 2017 where two or more companies work in collaboration on R&D projects under a cost-sharing arrangement. The definition of a cost-sharing arrangement will be narrowed and the way in which payments are structured under the cost-sharing arrangement will be altered. The changes will take effect from 1 April 2017.

Hybrid mismatches

FA 2016 introduced legislation to tackle aggressive tax planning involving the use of hybrid and other mismatch arrangements. It was announced in a technical note at Autumn Statement 2016 that two minor amendments would be made to the hybrid mismatch rules, and a TIIN has been published providing further details. The first change helps to relieve the administrative compliance burden in respect of financial instruments and the second change ensures that amortisation deductions are not treated as giving rise to a mismatch. The changes take effect from 1 January 2017.

Grassroots sports

It was originally announced at Autumn Statement 2015 that companies will be able to claim a deduction for contributions to grassroots sports in certain circumstances. It was announced today that the treatment of a sport governing body will be extended by Finance Bill 2017 to include its 100% subsidiaries. These provisions will have effect from 1 April 2017.

Tax relief for museums and galleries

As announced at Budget 2016, Finance Bill 2017 will introduce a new tax relief for museums and galleries. Further details on the operation of the relief were announced at Autumn Statement 2016. Following consultation on the legislation contained in draft Finance Bill 2017, it was announced today that the relief will be extended to allow for exhibitions which have a live performance as part of the exhibition, provided the live performance is not the main focus.

Corporation tax in Northern Ireland

For a number of years, the Government has been working with the Northern Ireland Executive to pursue the introduction of an Northern Ireland corporation tax rate of 12.5% from April 2018. It was confirmed today that all small and medium-sized enterprises trading in Northern Ireland will be given the potential to benefit. Anti-abuse provisions together with other minor drafting improvements will feature in the revised legislation contained in Finance Bill 2017.

Inheritance Tax, Trusts and Estates

The Spring Budget was light on new tax proposals overall, and inheritance tax did not feature at all. However, it is worth being reminded of some new measures due to be introduced with effect from April 2017 which have been previously announced and the budget included some new points relating to pensions and trusts which will be of interest to private client practitioners.

Trusts default rate of income tax

The OOTLAR, para 1.1 makes a somewhat cryptic reference to a 'default rate' of income tax which will apply to trustees. This is not a new rate of tax for trusts but requires some explanation.

With effect from 6 April 2017, the Scottish parliament will be able to set a Scottish rate of income tax to apply to non-savings, and non-dividend income in Scotland. This 'main rate' of tax will apply to individuals' employment, trade, pensions and property income. It does not apply to trusts.

To correspond with the creation of a main rate for Scottish taxpayers, the same term will apply to the non-savings, non-dividend income of individuals in the rest of the UK. The inference is, of course, that the main rates for each part of the UK could diverge in due course.

The regional authority over tax rates does not extend to the standard rates applied to trusts or non-residents. Hence the introduction of a new term, 'default rate' which describes the standard rate applied to non-savings, non-dividend income of those entities. For trusts, this category is primarily property income.

Although no additional measures are proposed at present, the separation of the rates does pave the way for different rates for trusts in the future.

Inheritance tax and the non-domicile rules

Practitioners are reminded that the Finance Bill 2017 will legislate for the reform of the domicile rules which was initially outlined in the Summer Budget 2015. The new rules will take effect from 6 April 2017. Draft legislation was published in January 2017 and the OOTLAR, para 1.26 confirmed that the measures will go ahead with only minor amendment. For inheritance tax purposes, the key changes are:

- a non-UK domiciled person (non-dom) will become deemed domiciled after being UK resident for 15 of the past 20 years (instead of 17 years out of 20 currently),
- a person with a UK domicile of origin who has acquired a different domicile of choice will be deemed domiciled while they are UK resident,

- inheritance tax will be charged on all UK residential property even when held by a non-dom through an offshore structure.

The standard non-dom tax planning strategy of placing foreign property in a non-UK resident trust before the individual becomes deemed domiciled continues to be an effective way of minimising UK tax, and is, in fact specifically confirmed in the OOTLAR and draft legislation. However, this strategy will no longer work for a non-dom who had a UK domicile of origin but becomes deemed domiciled when UK resident.

Inheritance tax and residence nil-rate band

For deaths after 6 April 2017 an increase in the nil-rate band will be available where the value of a residence is bequeathed to direct descendants.

VAT, other Indirect Taxes and Duties

VAT

Registration and deregistration thresholds

With effect from the 1 April 2017 the following thresholds will apply:

- VAT registration threshold will increase from £83,000 to £85,000.
- The VAT registration threshold for relevant acquisitions from other EU member states will also increase from £83,000 to £85,000.
- The VAT deregistration threshold will increase from £81,000 to £83,000.

Use and enjoyment provisions for business to consumer mobile phone services

The Government stated that it intends to remove the use and enjoyment provisions that alleviate the need for UK VAT to be charged on business to consumer (B2C) mobile phone services provided to a UK resident person travelling outside of the EU.

The change is intended to resolve the inconsistency where UK VAT is applied to mobile phones used by UK residents when in the EU, but not when the mobile phone is used outside the EU.

The changes are intended to prevent telecommunication providers from using the inconsistency to avoid accounting for UK VAT and it will bring the UK into line with the internationally agreed approach.

Secondary legislation and a TIIN will be published before the summer recess.

Fraud in the provision of labour in the construction sector

The Government announced that it intends to have a consultation on possible options to combat missing trader fraud in the provision of labour in the construction sector. One option would be to extend the scope of the domestic reverse charge mechanism to include labour provided in the construction industry so that the recipient accounts for any VAT due.

A consultation document will be published on 20 March 2017.

Split payment model

Certain overseas businesses avoid paying UK VAT on goods supplied online which undercuts UK retailers and abuses the trust of UK customers purchasing goods via an online marketplace.

The Government had previously announced the introduction of measures that are intended to combat VAT avoidance by online businesses in Autumn Statement 2016. The Government has now announced that it would like to collect evidence on whether it would be appropriate to introduce a new VAT collection mechanism in respect of online sales using technology that enables VAT to be collected and remitted directly to HMRC at the time the sale takes place.

This is commonly referred to as the split payment method, where the supplier will receive the net amount and the VAT will be remitted directly to HMRC. The Government believes that this will be another step that could be used to tackle VAT avoidance by overseas online suppliers selling goods to UK consumers.

A 'call for evidence' will be published on 20 March 2017.

Penalty changes in fraud cases

The Government announced in Autumn Statement 2016 that legislation will be included in Finance Bill 2017 introducing a penalty for participating in VAT fraud. The Government consulted on the draft legislation and as a result they have made some minor amendments to improve clarity of the measure and to limit the naming of a company officer to instances where the amount of tax due exceeds £25,000. The new penalty will come into effect from the date of Royal Assent to the Finance Bill.

Energy and transport taxes

Vehicle Excise Duty (VED)

The VED for cars, motorcycles and vans registered before 1 April 2017 will be increased by the Retail Price Index (RPI) with effect from 1 April 2017.

HGV VED and Road User Levy

These rates will be frozen with effect from 1 April 2017. The Government has requested evidence be provided in respect of updating the existing HGV Road User Levy and they will formally issue this request in Spring 2017. The Government also stated that it intends to work with the industry in order to update the levy so that it will reward hauliers that plan their routes efficiently and incentivise hauliers to make efficient use of the roads and improve air quality.

Red diesel

The Government announced that it intends to request evidence on the use of red diesel in order to improve its understanding of eligible industries and their use of red diesel. The Government would specifically like to receive evidence from urban red diesel users.

The call for evidence will be published on 20 March 2017.

Air Passenger Duty (APD)

The rate of APD for the year 2018/19 will increase in line with the RPI. The rates for 2019/20 will be provided in Autumn Budget 2017 in order to give airlines sufficient notice of the increase.

Carbon pricing

The Government announced that it remains committed to carbon pricing in order to assist with decarbonising the power sector. UK prices are currently determined by the EU Emissions Trading System and Carbon Price Support.

With effect from 2021/22, the Government intends to target a total carbon price and will set the specific tax rate at a later date in order to give businesses greater clarity on the total price that they will be required to pay. Further details on carbon prices for the 2020s will be set out at Autumn Budget 2017.

Levy control framework

The Government is aware that it will need to limit the cost for businesses and households as the UK decarbonises its energy supplies. The Levy Control Framework has already been assisting with controlling the costs of low carbon subsidies in recent years and it will be replaced by a revised set of controls. Details of these new controls will be provided later in 2017.

Insurance Premium Tax (IPT)

The Government has reconfirmed its announcement in Autumn Statement 2016 that it will be introducing anti-forestalling measures when the standard rate increases to 12% with effect from June 2017.

The current anti-forestalling legislation is no longer relevant so new legislation will be introduced with effect from 8 March 2017.

Under the anti-forestalling measure:

(a)   businesses will be required to charge the new rate of IPT on a premium received between the announcement and the rate change if the cover under the insurance contract starts on or after the date of the change. This is done by deeming the premium to be received on the date of the rate change. However, this does not apply where it is the insurer's normal commercial practice to receive pre-payments of premiums, and

(b)   businesses will be required to charge the new rate of IPT on a pro-portion of a premium received between the announcement and the rate change if the cover under the insurance contract starts before the rate change and extends until after the first anniversary of the rate change. This is done by deeming a proportion of the premium to be received on the rate change date. That proportion is the amount which relates to the period of cover which runs from the first anniversary. However, this does not apply where it is the insurer's normal commercial practice to issue contracts for periods longer than one year.

Environmental taxes

Aggregates levy

The current rate of £2 per tonne will remain in effect.

Landfill tax

The value of the Landfill Communities Fund (LCF) for 2017/18 will remain unchanged at £39.3m and the cap on contributions made by landfill operators will increase to 5.3%. The current cap will be maintained, subject to consideration of Landfill Tax receipts, continuing progress in reducing the level of unspent funds that are held by environmental bodies and the proportion of the LCF that are spent on administration costs.

The Government announced that it intends to consult on extending the scope of landfill tax to cover illegal waste disposals that are made without the required permit or licence.

Landfill tax – definition of taxable disposal

The Government previously announced at Budget 2016 that legislation will be introduced in Finance Bill 2017, and in secondary legislation, to amend the definition of a taxable disposal for landfill tax. The Government has consulted in the draft legislation and changes have been introduced in order to clarify the tax treatment of material disposed of at landfill sites and give greater certainty to landfill site operators. The draft legislation has been restructured to simplify and improve ease of comprehension. The measure will come into effect after Royal Assent to Finance Act 2017 and the changes will apply to disposals to landfill in England, Wales and Northern Ireland.

Alcohol and tobacco

Alcohol duty rates and bands

The duty rates on beer, cider, wine and spirits will increase by the RPI with effect from 13 March 2017.

The Government announced that it intends to have a consultation on:

(a) introducing a new duty band for still cider that has a just below 7.5% abv in order to target white ciders, and

(b) the impact of introducing a new duty band for still wine and made-wine between 5.5 and 8.5% abv.

Tobacco duty rates

The Government has previously announced in Budget 2014 that tobacco duty rates will increase by 2% above RPI inflation and this change will come into effect from 6pm on 8 March 2017.

Minimum Excise Tax

The Government announced that it will be introducing a Minimum Excise Tax for cigarettes that is intended to target the cheapest tobacco and promote fiscal sustainability. The rate will be set at £268.63 per 1,000 cigarettes. The new tax will come into effect from 20 May 2017.

Tobacco: Illicit Trade Protocol – licensing of equipment and the supply chain

Following the announcement made in Autumn Statement 2015 and following technical consultation on the draft legislation produced in December 2016, legislation will be introduced in Finance Bill 2017 that will be intended to control the use and ownership of tobacco manufacturing machinery in the UK. The changes are intended to prevent the illicit manufacture of tobacco products in the UK by introducing powers to establish a licensing regime for this type of machinery. Powers will also be introduced to provide for forfeiture of unlicensed tobacco manufacturing machinery and penalties for failure to comply with the conditions of a licence. The legislation will take effect from the date of Royal Assent.

Heated tobacco products

As announced in Budget 2016 the Government will be consulting on the duty treatment of heated tobacco products. The consultation will be launched on 20 March 2017 and the consultation document should be available on this date.

Soft drinks levy

The levy for sugar that is added to drinks with a total sugar content of at least five grams per 100 millilitres will be set at 18 pence per litre and drinks with a sugar content of at least eight grams will be set at 24 pence per litre. Manufacturers and importers who take reasonable steps to reduce the sugar content will pay less or alleviate the need to pay the levy at all.

Following consultation the legislation has been revised to include a criminal offence for evasion of the levy. Minor amendments have also been made to improve clarity. The levy will take effect from April 2018.

Gaming duty

Gross gaming yield (GGY)

The Government previously announced in Budget 2016 that they will include legislation in Finance Bill 2017 that will raise the GGY bandings for Gaming Duty in line with inflation based on the RPI. The revised GGY will be used to calculate the amount of Gaming Duty due for accounting periods starting on or after 1 April 2017.

Remote gaming duty – freeplays

The Government announced in Budget 2016 that it will include legislation in Finance Bill 2017 to amend the definition of gaming payment and prizes and change the tax treatment of freeplays for remote gaming duty. The Government consulted on the changes and the draft legislation has been amended to ensure that the change is proportionate. The legislation is intended to ensure that freeplays used to participate in remote gaming will have a value as stakes when calculating the dutiable profit of the operator and freeplays given as prizes will not be deductible.

Anti-Avoidance

Promoters of Tax Avoidance Schemes (POTAS)

The Government announced that it intends to introduce new legislation that is intended to ensure that promoters of tax avoidance schemes cannot circumvent the new POTAS regime by reorganising their business to either share control of a promoting business or putting persons between the promoting business and themselves.

Strengthening tax avoidance sanctions and deterrents

The Government previously announced in Autumn Statement 2016 that a new penalty will be introduced in respect of a person who has enabled another person or business to use a tax avoidance arrangement that is later defeated by HMRC. The Government also intends to remove the defence of having relied on non-independent advice as taking reasonable care when HMRC considers whether penalties will be levied on a person or business that has used a tax avoidance arrangement.

The changes relating to reasonable care come into effect at Royal Assent and apply to inaccuracies in documents relating to tax periods which begin on or after 6 April 2017. The penalty for enablers will apply prospectively to enabling activity after Royal Assent.

Disclosure of indirect tax avoidance schemes

The Government announced in Autumn Statement 2016 that legislation will be introduced in Finance Bill 2017 that is intended to strengthen the regime for disclosing indirect tax avoidance arrangements. The provisions will make scheme promoters primarily responsible for disclosing schemes to HMRC and the scope of the legislation will be extended to include all indirect taxes including the Soft Drinks Levy. These measures will become effective from 1 September 2017.